ANCHOR BOOKS

Love's Many Pathways

Edited by

Sarah Marshall

First published in Great Britain in 2005 by
ANCHOR BOOKS
Remus House,
Coltsfoot Drive,
Peterborough, PE2 9JX
Telephone (01733) 898102

SB ISBN 1 84418 397 1

FOREWORD

Anchor Books is a small press, established in 1992, with the aim of promoting readable poetry to as wide an audience as possible.

We hope to establish an outlet for writers of poetry who may have struggled to see their work in print.

The poems presented here have been selected from many entries, and as always editing proved to be a difficult task.

I trust this selection will delight and please the authors and all those who enjoy reading poetry.

Sarah Marshall
Editor

CONTENTS

You And He!

Ashes strewn upon the Earth
How life dashes since one's birth
Gone to Heaven with He above
Gone from me - the one I love
Moved by breeze that often blows
What she's thinking no one knows
All I know is that I be
Broken hearted without she
Hurt is calming as time flies
I remember - smile in eyes
Ashes strewn upon the ground
There's some solace I have found
Not the gloom nor am morose
While I am here now very close
There are flowers - strewn around
Where she lies in disturbed ground
Give her the peace that she deserves
And some for me to calm the nerves
As I must go once I have prayed
I hope she won't be then dismayed
I will return from whence I came
To join my love right here - again
I wish that I could be more bold
I wish that too she I could hold
To feel the beat of gentle heart
Not this hate that we're apart
Dear loving God please ease the pain
Promise me - we will meet again
Goodbye love, you I adore
I see you now - as was before!
I see the smile that lit your face
You're here with me through his dear grace!

Jackdaw

Sands Of Time

I walk alone across the sand,
Where we once walked hand in hand,
Together you and me,
But now my tears are echoed by the sea.

The ghostly sounds of yesteryear,
Our happy voices I still hear,
The distant memories of misspent youth,
High spirits, loud laughter, so uncouth.

So many years have now gone by,
The carefree love's grown strong,
Deep within our hearts entwine our souls,
To each we now belong.

The seagulls haunting cry above,
Tells all who hear, of our true love.

Now my footsteps span the years,
Sweet memories bring smiles, and tears,
For my love now you are gone,
And I walk these sands alone.

C V Perkins

Pierced Lightning

I cried for 20 minutes as the lightning pierced the sky
I hugged the pillow when the thunder crashed
I whispered your name as it pelted with rain
I bowed my head as the power went down
I wished you were here as the headlights of pain glare through
The twilight black sky
I hope you're the light at the end of the tunnel.

Paul Davies

Time Catches Up!

Life's shattered, world in tatters
Lost the people, whom really matter
Taken away from home, to another
Being looked after by others
Here a very peaceful place
Away from the hectic race
Never wanted here from the beginning
Waiting for family and friends to call
Not a lot to wish for
New homes not far
To see them would bring joy
Special treat feel in store
Knowing they've not changed at all
Certainly pleasing face to face see
Even regular visiting, be lovely
Communication needing
Letter's still able to read, write too
Why phone call, can't visit you
Again to wait promise call
Old age, with sickness
Catches up with us all.

Rosemary Sheridan

Grandparents' House

Steel coats of mail, in the driest cabinet
In the place where all others have moulded and crumbled.
Where two ghosts have stood and communicated arcanely.
Where the construction of their reciprocal mirror came to fruition
And where there is a damp spot . . . yet tranquillity
In the domestic interior under consideration.

M Courtney Soper

THERE FOR ME

If tears could build a stairway to my loved ones up above
Then I would be so happy to take them all my love
I'd kiss my mum and hug my dad and tell them, 'I've missed you'
And just to see them standing there would be a dream come true.

When I was young I never dreamt that life could be so sad
Taking things for granted not knowing what I had.
Enjoying every day that came with happiness around
Now everything is quiet I long to hear their sound.

The memories I have of them are fond and full of fun
Everything they had they'd give and it was gladly done.
We shared a lot of happy times although the days were hard
They never let me go without a smile was their reward.

But I can cope because I know that they can see and hear
And that when I'm in trouble they'll chase away my fear.
They'd never ever leave me, I'm their child and they both care
And when my time is over, they'll both be waiting there.

Elizabeth McNeil

YOU

You were in the sun just now
Not in the shade.
You were in the games playing
Not the ones played.
You're everywhere good
And nowhere bad.
Remembering your happiness
Makes me sad.

I miss you.

Maureen Thomas

Bob White And The Whip-Poor-Will

They sing their solemn songs when night is not far on . . .
Their solitary tunes sing of a memory long gone . . .
A memory most distant and yet, it seems so near
And summons up a plethora of hopes and dreams and fears.
The porch that wraps around the house
That holds things from the past . . .
The treasures from a life ago,
The things, through life, that last . . .
The kitchen, so resplendent . . .
Dark halls, steeped in mystery . . .
Long winding stairs - which go nowhere
The child in us won't seek
In cloistered, musty parlours,
Are chairs with strong, straight backs . . .
The once bright mirrors, shining,
Though dulled by seasons past . . .
The sunset on a childhood, which great, unnoticed then -
Is only now remembered as one's life comes
Near its end
I long to hear the Bob White
Sing his song among the fields . . .
And his old friend, the whip-poor-will,
Cry out among the hills . . .
The memories that linger - the memories that last,
Are made of stuff we've conjured up
In dreams and from the past.

Deborah Gail Pearson

HEARTACHE

So many years they lived together
Now, only photographs remain,
Nothing now will be the same
Life is a different game.

So many years they laughed together
Now, mere silence exists there,
Seeing that empty old chair
No one around to care.

So many years they cried together
Now, she weeps on her own,
The garden now overgrown
If only she had known.

So many years they worked together
Now, every day is too long,
She is no longer as strong
Why did it all go wrong?

So many years they played together
Now, the games have ended,
Indefinitely suspended
Heartache extended.

So many years they loved together
Now, only loneliness can win,
Those memories stay within
Her head begins to spin.

So many years they were together
Now, those times slowly fade,
Their music is never played
No dancing in the arcade.

George S Johnstone

A Drinking Binge

I was persuaded to go out for a drink or two,
The reason I went was because I was feeling so lonely
After suddenly losing you.
You were my life, my body and my soul,
My one true love and we were always together
And we had a ball.
But you were killed fighting in a far-off land,
And no longer will I be able to hold your hand.
I went down to the pub with some friends of mine
Drowning my sorrows; I drank a lot of wine.
Then came the gin, whiskey, vodka and rum,
I'm now addicted to the bottle by gum.

I tried to find some comfort in the drink,
Then all my friends made me think,
What am I doing, I know it is wrong but where can I go,
Where do I belong?
They tell me my body's in a mess, my liver is failing,
And I'm being told by my doctor who is Tess.

I have met someone new and he has pulled me out of the blue,
He makes me happy just like you used to do.
My body is now mending, my liver is new,
My life is a lot better by far,
And my new husband Dave is my bright shining star,
We have three children, twin boys and a girl.
And my future is a bright, shining pearl,
We are one happy family Dave, our children and me,
But I still cry a tear or two sometimes when I think of you,
I know that you're in Heaven on high,
And my life went to pieces on the day you did die,
You'll never know how much I did cry after losing you
That way I nearly died,
But I now have a happy family and I know in your heart
You will forgive me.

R Muir

THE FINAL MAP

who would have thought
I'd need an ordinance map
to take my grieving mother
to Ullapool's silver bell
of mist and forgetfulness?

she nods and withdraws
past the aching scenery

Crainlarich boredom
Glencoe cold sigh

as bitter roads straighten
the thick arterial lines
red routes of separation
unfold, unfold, unfold

avoided minor towns
the cut right through
heart stopping snow
bottomless loch detour
moor and sucking want
the lost and never had

the past is granite brown
whorls of hurt blood
and purple iodine crusts

I try arranging a forest
of sorry green in her lap
but a geometry of creases
she has ironed in place
cannot be folded back

I drive on cautiously
although there's no point
or happy destination

no survey map of grief
can guide me back
to the childhood home
she used to safeguard
behind frightened eyes

Robin Lindsay Wilson

Butterfly Bright Eyes

I sit, silent, weeping unseen tears,
aloneness turning to solitude
when, with a gentle flutter butterfly
bright eyes wink on my hand -

a butterfly . . .

I left you, still warm
leaving you a part of my heart.
The empty flat more desolate
without your padding paws. Quietly
a soft shimmer of wings breezed by
alighting on your empty bed.
The hollowed cream rug
adorned by peacock beauty;
bright blue seeing my tears.

The butterfly stayed 'til morning,
and disappeared as
your spirit returned
to stay for a while . . .

watching over me
until with love, I set you free . . .

Anita Richards

PARIS PICTURE

From a 5th floor Paris room,
I look out,
As a Lowry picture comes to life
Before me.
In the distance,
Smoke pours from factory chimneys towards the north.
Tall buildings pierce the sky,
While down below,
Pristine white and turquoise
Metro trams cross the iron bridge,
Every few minutes.
In the street,
People constantly come and go.
Visit and depart from la Poste
Opposite.
Stride purposefully along the boulevard,
Or cluster at the bus stop.
A group grows,
The bus arrives and sucks them in.
The shelter is empty,
Until one by one,
A new group forms.
This Lowry picture
Constantly changes.
Everyone is in transit.
Only I remain still,
Watching.

Meg Cheeseman

Goodbye To Nan

The day had arrived
to say goodbye
knowing that we
would surely cry

Our flowers were ordered
and a message we wrote
telling Nan how we felt
in a short note

We followed her into church
our tears just flowed
The memories we had
and the grief we showed

The service was lovely
My poem was read
We listened to the vicar
and all that he said

We went to the cemetery
That goodbye was our last
as I threw in a rose
I thought of her past

You'll be in our hearts forever
We will always love you
Goodbye from us all Nan
and watch over us too.

Vicky Willis

Every Seven Years, I Change

Every seven years, I change.
Lots of love and kisses, nothing was missing,
Ponytails, fairy tales, ghost stories were told,
Then no more grandparents, as they just got so old.

Every seven years, I change.
Lots of laughter and tears, as we all got dafter,
Bonfires, football, cricket and other things,
Then no more players, they just got so old.

Every seven years, I change.
Lots of pubs, nightclubs and boyfriends galore,
Gangs of us stood, the crowd begging for more,
Then we all moved on because we all got so old.

Every seven years, I change.
To tell you the truth, we all welcomed the rest,
Safe in the knowledge, we gave it our best,
Then we all moved on because we all got so old.

Julie Walker-Daniel

My Vermont's Friend

My American e-friend Nancy Monroe,
loves swimming, camping, dancing and even snow.
Hobbies, she collects, as she tells
are lighthouses, angels, cats/dogs and sea shells.

Brother, two sisters, daughter and two sons,
grandchildren of three are so much fun.
Vermont is pretty in the fall, I've been told,
I would love to see it, before I am too old.

What a very merry friend indeed she is and I am told very bold.

Barry Ryan

TAKING JAMES TO THE PARK

Yvonne arrived a little bit flustered
and asked if I could look after him.
I thought Jesus you must be desperate,
I can't look after *myself,* but warmed
to the idea, especially as
the expression on his face suggested
he really couldn't care less.

After ten minutes getting no response, I asked
did he like the ducks, he shook his head
in exasperation to tell me I knew nothing.
They were quack-quacks. I put him on
the swing, the slide, the life-support machine
and the roundabout littered with debris,
still thinking of those vivid mandarin
colours and trying to recover from

being put in my place; Jennie did this
to me so often. Auf wiedersehen,
I'd say: immediately she'd tell me
I'd been watching *Heidi,* asked me about
an abstract painting and I said it's just
like when you make patterns. I can see
a cat in it, she insists and, puzzled, I ask
where she gets a cat from. She tells me
a pet shop and her mum collapses.

I point out a mistle thrush and all
he comes out with is *bic-bic,* like Nick crying
weem for ice cream whenever he hears
the chimes of the van. *Bic-bic,* I thought
as I parked him outside the shop; rewarded him
with a couple of indelible pens.

John Rafferty

My Gran

My gran - what can I say,
She is still with me every day.
Me, just a small girl in my Sunday best,
And she, rubbing goose grease on my chest.
'Have you got on your liberty vest?'

She loved my golden curls, and me
And would make me crumpets for my tea.
'Eat what's in front of you,' she would say,
'Or no more food till the following day.'

The end of the war was a difficult time
But Gran would always come up with a rhyme.
If you wanted to dream it wasn't a sin
But Gran would say, 'One day our boat will come in.'

She always left a little food in the pan
And maybe, the odd slice of ham.
If any tramps passed our house that day,
She would feed them, then send them on their way.

She was mayoress of a ship-building town
And would go to a 'do' in a fine handmade gown.
She made all my dresses so pretty and neat
And a coat for a princess that fitted a treat.

She had rickets as a child, but her bandy legs
Carried her far and wide,
Pushing a trolley round the hospital ward,
She may have been seventy, but never got bored.

She would chase naughty dog 'Tim' when he wouldn't stay
And went to roll in a field quite a long way away.
When he came back, she would smack him a lot,
But he still wagged his tail, and resumed his 'posh trot'.

My gran - she really taught me a lot,
She had morals and standards, but harsh she was not.
I loved her so much from cradle to grave,
With her wisdom I thought the world she could save.

I think with her strength, she 'saved' quite a few
I have always thought she knows what I do
With my children, I've lived my life, best that I can
But could never be quite as 'great' - as my gran.

Jennifer H Fox

Moments

That's a lovely wall with the sun on it.
If I took a bouncy tennis ball,
As once I would, and shot it
At the wall, how satisfying
Is the sound? Or, if I painted it
Upon a canvas, as once I might,
How rich the colours, reddish brick
On patchy white attractively peeling,
Texture rough, budleia in crevasses,
And the old willow tree draping
His dress, brushing the top
And stealing the sun into ochre shade
With braid on braid of pale green fringes,
How peaceful!

Some soothing things that still remain
To flee to, calming moments
In the rush and change, made
To remember. Always!

Diane Burrow

Talking On The Telephone

Please somebody phone up for a chat,
I long for the telephone ringing,
Did Mum ever find her little lost cat?
How's Natania getting on with her singing?
Has Julie any word on moving to Spain?
Their lives are always changing,
Janet's on the move again.
Her life she is now rearranging,
I usually hear from Greg much more,
But lately there's no news,
Lorna always knows the score
And passes on her views.
Lee and Ryan don't need to phone,
They drop in every day,
Lee stays ten minutes, then goes home,
But Ryan prefers to stay.

J Hagen

Daddy

(Dedicated to my dad)

It broke my heart the day you left
It made me cry, I was so bereft.
I was just a kid when you did part
It left me with a broken heart.
Up to the heavens God took you that day
I couldn't think straight and could only pray
That together we would be and forever stay
In Heaven how good that would be
Where once again I could sit upon your knee.
Oh Daddy dear how I miss you so
Why did you have to leave me?
Why did you have to go?

Maggie Strong

CHRISTMAS PAST

(Dedicated to my nan, Pearl Evans)

At Christmas time we would gather
Round our nan's house
For a party.
The adults would chat,
While us children, huddled
Round the food table,
Whispering and giggling.

The noises were deafening;
Laughter,
Talking.
The piano could be heard,
Bringing melodies in-between the monotones.

The clock ticked on,
Us children would be put to bed,
Top-to-toe,
Whilst the adults continued
In their 'festive jollities'.

The morning dawned,
Each family would go,
Their separate ways,
For another year.

The years have turned into decades,
And Nan is no longer here,
My memories of those times together,
Will stay with me for evermore.

Debbie Nobbs

CALLING FOR HELP

Our baby girl was dying, seizing with convulsions
And a permanent croup.
I was told, 'Watch, feed and nurse her at home.'
I held her, I fed her and prayed day and night,
Yet she grew weaker hour by hour.

Exhausted, I sat, holding her tight,
It grew dusk and the other little ones
Crowded around. What could they do?
One brought a book, another an engine and the other
A black and white panda.

Suddenly, there was a light
Or was it a shadow?
A tall figure bent over us
And took from my arms
The little scrap of human distress.
I couldn't speak, yet knew we were safe
The figure was kind and smiled at us all.
I suddenly knew him -
My father who died in the war,
Had never known grandchild,
But had answered my call.

I woke a while later, the children played on
And the little one - asleep in her cot!
Next day, both doctor and nurse, astonished, declared,
'She's over the crisis, we see.'

Death is never the end of a life, I know, I believe and I've seen.
We've guardians beyond like my pa
Who'll come in our hour of desperate need.

Georgina Treeves

THE SILENT VOICE

(For Nanette Sylvia Neal)

Listen to me
Now don't you cry
Be strong for yourself
Hold your head up high
Go out and show the world
That you can live
Live life to the full
Because you can have it all.

Listen to me
You are strong inside
I'll hold your hand
All through the night
Go out and get what you want
I know you can
Grab life with both hands
Just don't lose your dreams.

I'm the wind beneath your wings
I'll carry you along
When you call out my name
You'll find I'll never be gone
I'm the guide you look for inside
I'm your inspiration
Go out and make me proud
Scream and shout so loud
Make yourself heard
Live life to the full
I'm the wind beneath your wings
I'll carry you along.

Helen Popple

My Dearest Love

I'll see you in Pitlochry,
Where the salmon leap
Where the mist rolls off the mountains
Where the hills are filled with sheep
I'll see you when I watch the stream
Flow steadily along
Till it merges with a mighty roar
Making its own sweet song
I'll see you as the sun shines
Through a watery sky
I'll stand and watch the rainbow
And then I'll wonder why
Two people who had everything
Could throw it all away
Instead of helping each other
Through their 'rainy day'
Their children too have suffered
The pain has left its mark
When realisation has set in
The reality is stark
For now our 'strife' is over
Life's sweet again once more
But alas, my dearest love,
This play has no encore

Janet Robertson Jones

The Empty Chair

All the thoughts we never
made real,
all the words and the dreams
we steal,
make no illusion out of an
empty chair . . .

your life is nowhere to be found,
the voice in my head remains
the merest echo of you . . .
as the dust settles, and the
windows give their midnight
moan . . .

I remember you moving
through the darkness near the bed,
the sheets forget the picture
of you there
sitting in the empty chair . . .

The night makes deliberate
noises . . . just to confuse,
memories of you made
into mimicry . . .
they unite to defeat hope,
and visions of you sitting in the empty chair . . .

Peter Maher

FINAL PARTING

There he lay
A collection of twigs
Against the snow of sheets
In the drab room
That had no connection with warmth and home
Or life, which like his flesh
Was melting fast away,

The days and hours departed,
Marked only by the insistent hiss of the device
Pressing morphine
Into pained flesh.

Then I wanted him to go
As I'd wanted him to walk away
Long ago from trains 'now departing'
Not to prolong the awkward goodbye.

But he left me by degrees.
We talked and he was
My father still.

And then the next day
Fluttering hands illustrating
Some point half-remembered
In a meeting long ago adjourned
Poignantly preoccupied
With some small old frustration
Still unresolved.

Poison or the drugs
Corroding his mind
And he was gone and yet
Still clinging to life.
I did not recognise him but even so
Clung onto the fact
That he was there.

Yet wanting it to end.
And at the last breath I wanted him back
With all my heart,
The final parting
Impossible, after all, to bear.

Jenny Donnison

ARIDITY

I have been away, dear Lord,
My heart and soul elsewhere,
(But then, You knew that!)

Lost awhile amid mists,
Swirling shapes, covering, uncovering.

I knew not where I was,
Only that I could not find You.
(God, how I missed You.)

A little time, perhaps,
To find myself again:
And You, dear Lord,
Who never let me leave from Your sight.

Home once more.

You ask no questions, no explanations.

Lord, it is good to be home.
To be at one.
To hold You.

John M Beazley

WONDER YEARS

Watching the sun go down on the dusk of adolescent days,
Memories of another day, some engraved, some erased.
'Tis the magical twilight hour and so you shall gaze,
Westward, enthralled by the sunset's golden haze.
Turn east, menacing clouds loom in the distance, but be bold.
You'll learn to spot the silver lining, and you'll strike gold.
It will be a night filled with stars a million and the moon.
Dreams are many and are free, just don't wake up too soon.
Then you hear the lark herald the advent of the morn,
You will open your eyes and wake up to adulthood's dawn,
The sunset, the twilight, the stars and the moon, all gone,
The radiance of the rising sun is far more, you are reborn.
You will then remember what you dreamt of, all night long.
'Dreams are meant to be pursued', so you will carry on . . .

Prasad Rajendran

GRANDPARENTS

G iving always your best
R easoning that life is full of tests
A dvancing in age, you never quiver
N urturing gives you full pleasure
D eep love you give unwaveringly
P arental guidance give us nourishment
A greement to disagree never a hindrance
R eminisce, you did plenty of
E njoyment of laughter - that's what we're after
N ever forgetting your undying love
T reasuring your wisdom
S urely your love cannot be brought at any cost

Angela Nevo Hopkins

Old Faithful Friend

My old faithful friend
Went to the Heavens above
He showed me such loyalty
And gave me much love

Then the time came
When I had to let him go
My heart filled with pain
How I loved him so

I didn't want to do it
But you were very ill
My eyes are so sore
With the tears that they fill

I remember all the walks we had
And how you loved to run
We had some good laughs
And lots and lots of fun

The house seems so empty
The garden so bare
Life can be so cruel
And very unfair

You used to always protect me
And wouldn't let anyone come near
You'd only have to turn your head
With your menacing looking stare

I feel ever so guilty
But what could I have done
I am so sorry with all my heart
My beautiful brown eyed son

Gillian Barrett

Missing You

I know you've only gone away
And I'll be seeing you again someday
We're so close, yet so far apart
I miss you so much, even though you're in my heart

I remember all the times we used to argue
Over the tiniest things that never ever mattered
And in the end, neither of us won
Because we'd forgotten the point of our bantering

I remember when you got me from the school gates
I'd run into your arms, and you'd spin me around
I'd tell you about my good days
And you made me forget the bad

I remember our shopping trips to the mall
We'd shop and shop till our feet bled and hurt
Trying on clothes, and buying little charms
And we always stopped for a drink and ice cream

I remember my boyfriends would come and go
You were there all the time, right by my side
When I was with them, you waited at home
And when we broke up, you had biscuits ready

I miss our arguing
I miss seeing your face at the end of the day
I miss spending money with you
I miss falling back on you
I miss your jokes, your hugs, your smile
And most of all, I miss your love

I know you've only gone away
And I'll be seeing you again someday

Anya Lees

Wax

From the beginning
As you walked through the door
Epitome of my fantasy
Not sure how to play you

Are you smarter than me?
Touch is more powerful than words
Touch and words together
Meant to look playful
Deeper meaning, look for it

Shame you had to be drunk
When you told me I'm lovely
Mouth open expectant
Cold hands on my body

My mind cannot switch off
What happens now?
It's forgotten
Put to one side

What was once
Consuming
Nauseating lust
Is now cooling wax
Hardening, to become cold and brittle
You are standing ready, axe in hand
Poised to shatter me

Break my heart
Turn my blood into vapour
Let me be carried into the sky
If you cannot see me
I do not exist.

Sara Pyefinch

Shadows On The Lawn

Moonbeams glide across the lawn,
Kissing its plush velvet
As they steal towards the sundial.

Herbaceous borders turn to silver
As scented flowers distil soft moonlight;
And as the shadow cast by the gnomon
Creeps by degrees across the lawn
I become aware of the passing of time -
Time that will never return.

And now, as night exudes exquisite fragrances,
Something I can scarcely define
Rises from the lawn, from the play of shadows -
Something which stirs my heightened fancy.
Is it a figment of my imagination?
Or is it a ghostly form that gropes
Towards me, octopus arms outstretched?
I feel a touch upon my forehead -
A whispered caress, nothing more.

The moment passes like a dream,
And all is still.
Only the divine murmur of a brook
Sings to me from hushed woods nearby
As I drink night's draught
And turn to go indoors,
Remembering.

It's exactly ten years
Since she passed away;
And during that time
I've never forgotten
Her last embrace
By the sundial,
That touch upon my forehead -
That whispered caress.

Robert D Hayward

FREEFALL

freefall on restless silent wings
as the eagle soars in golden silence
the sweet defiant nightingale softly sings
with unsung dreams of self reliance

feathered clouds packed full with rain
luminous rainbow coloured bright
rendered tales of sorrow and pain
while flying wings unleash the open kite

in tender arms they fall with grace
entangles hopes defy
sweet air's reliant and hope's embrace
god's trusting love to deny

high flying birds weep wail and cry
the rainbow hales of woe
lost diving lords of the sky
in howling depths of the sea below

A Copland

I THOUGHT I COULD FORGET YOU

I thought I could forget you
When we said our last goodbye
This I found impossible
I cannot live a lie.

I'll love you forever
And think of you all the time
One day we'll be as one
And I will make you mine.

Fate brought us together
On that beautiful day
Our eyes met your tender smile
I love you I want you to say.

Only time will tell
If our love is really true
But I know in my heart
I cannot live without you.

David Sheasby

THE END

I've tasted where I'm going
And it tasted so good
I've seen my angel.
She's where my resting place is
She's where my pain ends
She's my last road
Sorry for whom I leave behind
I've found my place
My time is coming
To be with my angel of life
Goodbye.

Pamela Massey

FULL MOON

The flickering stars light up the night sky
A full moon catches your silhouette
Memories from the past, things that have been.

Silence engulfs my head
Even the noise of the early morning streets
Are unable to remove this feeling of emptiness.

My heart misses a beat,
Just thinking of your name
The pain flows through my limbs
Numbing my fingers and toes.

Dawn, and my eyes adjust
To the bright light of morning
The vision of you has gone
And all I can do is hope
For another full moon.

G Clayton

GIRLS JUST WANT TO HAVE FUN

Simple days, inspired, delighted,
again and again I watched, in a fantasy,
believing myself to be there.

Smiling, wanting, sensing,
re-enacting. It was in my veins.

Sixteen annual celebrations, charging
through each year, never-ever forgetting.
Never wanting to forget.

With an adult press of 'Play' and
a nostalgic thrill
I'm 10 years old all over again!

Susan Macdougal

Regrets

When we look back,
O'er the years since our birth,
Where have they gone
And what were they worth?

Have we been wise
In the time we have spent
Using our talents,
In the way we were meant.

Have we been side-tracked?
Has time passed us by?
Did we use every minute
Not wisely, then why?

We're always so busy,
Rushing round everywhere,
Hither and thither,
No time left to spare.

Somehow the years,
Just seem to have flown,
Bad years, sad years,
And good years we've known.

Soon comes the time,
When we all must take stock,
Before we hear,
The last tick of the clock.

Anne E Hutchinson

You And I

What's happened to the boy I knew
When I was five and you were two
We shared such laughter, joy and fun
But now it seems those days are done.

I wonder if you really know
How much it hurts to let this go
The closeness that we shared before
We both grew up and closed the door.

Upon our happy carefree days
They all appear as just a haze
Oh how I long for them once more
Why can't we open up the door.

We both are older now you see
And life has moulded you and me
Sometimes I wonder who we are
This road has taken us too far.

If we could look beyond the hurt
We caused each other with words so curt
I'm sure we'd find forgiveness there
To heal, so we may once again share.

Those happy moments long ago
They're waiting there, this I know
And the boy as well who I once knew
When I was five and you were two.

S Ward

Two Names

Two boys first became friends in nineteen-o-three:
Two boys late that summer carved their names on a tree:
Two names of two boys to carefree to know
If roughly or smoothly their life paths would go.
For them at that moment an era was born;
A child age, no ice age or Bronze Age could scorn.
Bird nesting, no resting, so much to be done:
One carried a camera to capture the fun.
Walking and talking then sitting and wishing,
Praying and playing a line out when fishing.
No thoughts in their minds of this ever ending
Till one emigrated, 'Bon Voyage' so heart rending.
Now never to meet, now never to speak
But letters and photos exchanged by the week.
And boys of their fathers soon fathers of boys
So Christmas and birthdays they always sent toys.
A world in-between but still sharing so much,
This was the routine that kept them in touch.
Familiar patterns of family life,
Some children, a home, a hearth and a wife.

Then news from abroad of the end of a friend;
A lifetime of memories now brought to an end,
Just leaving some photos, some letters and me
And two faded boys' names carved on a tree.

Paul Denver

Christmas Dreams

I sit alone,
The air heavy with hazed memories of laughter,
Nostalgia, dead now to the past.
I see your face, smiling, close to mine;
Secret whispers, giggles reserved for you and me.
They never did quite understand,
They never did really see what lit those smiles,
I don't remember now, it all seems so dead.

The ancient Christmas tree
Threadbare with generations of love,
Shows me the gateway to a past, so warm.
I can see it smile,
Relaying recollections mirrored in the baubles,
Reflected in the firefly lights.

How we laughed,
We thought we could take on the world,
We thought we were unbeatable;
You and me against eternity.
Baby photos, children playing,
Smiles immortalised behind glass.

Their faces distort,
Sucked into the whirlpool of time.
You are gone, all is gone.
But still the loyal Christmas tree remains,
Your smile reflected forever in the lights,
And your laughter, heavy, in the air.

Alyson Pavitt (15)

PRESENTS FOR SAFIQA

I'd like to give her beautiful blue irises
if she were with me now.
And a box of plain chocolates, sticky, sweet and brown.
I'd stand with her under the stars and silvery moon.
And walk through Chorlton Water Park with her in the
shimmering sun.
And go to the seaside in Blackpool with her
where I used to go as a child with Grandma and have fun.
Or travel on a boat.
Take her belly dancing.
I'd let her wear my blue coat.
I'd buy her a CD she likes by Shaggy.
And we could watch The Sound of Music together,
and I'd like to say to this person 'I miss you more than ever.'

Rachel Van Den Bergen

ANOTHER LOVE

I cannot love another
And no one can take your place

Every time I close my eyes
I can only see your face

Wishing I was there with you
Laying side by side

For you I must tell all my hopes and dreams
And swallow all my pride

There cannot be the two of us
In this moment in time

But being here without you
Proves love is just a crime.

Lisa Miller

WOULDST THOU WALK

Wouldst thou walk with me my love,
Amidst the dew with stars above,
Let me take thy hand and talk,
Of love and life as oft we walk,
Through lush green grass and fields of blue,
And let me tell of love for you.

Wouldst thou walk with me my dear,
While I confess my darkest fear,
The thought of life without you close,
Doth make me sad and most morose,
Wilt thou hold and comfort me,
As I enfold my arms round thee?

Wouldst thou walk with me my sweet,
And tread my path with thine own feet,
As through this life we tread with care,
Wilt thou stay with me to share,
Through saddened times, contented bliss,
What canst thou say, my love, to this?

Séan James Olson

CHEMISTRY

You're not even my type, so dedicated, unproud
I'm a class A babe, gorgeous, wild, loud
Quiet chemist with counter, you tend others' pain
Yet gently ignore me to drive me insane.

Must I feign illness, will you be my cure?
Or would you advise on some intimate wound?
OK - I'll faint on the shop floor from frustration and strife
You'll be forced to revive me
With your kiss of life.

Maggie Amelia Nixon

MEMORIES OF 1942

I hear the planes fly overhead as I lie nightly in my bed
I know from engine sounds they make and by directions that they take
whether they are friend or foe as on their deadly way they go
Perhaps they've been across the sea
blasting others, such as we and are now returning home
tired and weary, having flown, for hours from some forsaken place
where once were buildings, now just space
If they're foe and visiting us carrying fire and noise, and just
the other day I heard the sound of bombs, without regard
dropped on people, kids and all in Belswains Lane, quite near
the school
But this an isolated case, dropped in error, or in haste
no target here that I could see, just a railway and a factory
In daylight too, the other day I saw a 'Dogfight' in the sky
this was in the afternoon, one day in the middle of June
Dornier Bombers, flying high and Spitfires trying to destroy
The cannon fire was loud and clear
and the scream of engines seemed quite near
as I watched in awe, neck strained back
as the Spitfires mounted their attack
I was out delivering bread that day in Deaconsfield Road, I have to say
and taking loaves to Mrs Floyd, knocking her door, which was
open wide
no one came, but a voice replied, from the garden,'Want to come inside,
take cover in the shelter here until the siren sounds, all clear?'
'No thanks,' I said, 'I must push on,
lots to do and they'll soon be gone,' scrapping there up in the sky,
moving all the time away, away from sight and soon from sound
as though they'd never been around.

John Gilbert Slade

Still

I still think about you every minute of every day,
memories of happy times spent together refusing to fade or die

If only you had told me long ago that my love was unrequited
you would have saved me much heartache

Now I am in turmoil, broken hearted, trying to erase
you from my mind without success

Don't think I will ever forget you because I fell so heavily.
Never have I experienced a love this strong.
It has penetrated so deeply that it flows like blood
through my veins

Before your bombshell all my thoughts and actions were directed
towards you. But, now, my life has no direction and I wander
around aimlessly, in a daze, like a zombie

Maybe, one day, someone will tap me on the shoulder
and say, hey, it's all been a bad dream

But, no, this has all been real, too real, like an out of control
roller coaster ride to oblivion and now I need to be strong
and deal with it

Problem is I remain as intensely in love with you as ever
and have no strength left to fight my feelings.
I have a delete key on my computer but it won't delete love

I still think about you every minute of every day,
still dream of what might have been . . .

Nash

THEN AND NOW

God! I will pack and take a train to get me to Cardiff
once again
For Cardiff's one place I know where folks with praying
hearts could go
Cardiff was beyond dispute the Premier Port in the world for the
Export of coal - hooters and whistles could be heard day and night
From ships and trains and planes in flight.
It is certainly true - a shop on every street corner -
they never gave up - there they stayed until taken up -
there was a cobbler, a barber, a grocer, bike mender, a chip shop
or pawnshop. If you had something to tender.
The lads after work would whistle and sing
Cor! A night at the pictures was having a fling -
if they saw a cowboy picture, Charlie Chaplin thrown in,
It was six pence well spent to have a good grin
Now here I am the last of six - two of my brothers lived on ships,
Cardiff hailed a nautical school where lads went
from their local school, after completing a four year course
they awaited a call to the sea.
There were hard times, sad times, troubles galore,
little did we think they would survive a war,
but thinking of our home, our family, our love,
they were now on the bridge and could thank God above.
Gone are the hooters, the ships, the docks, the area has a new name,
'The Bay' with an opera house to come so they say.
Those were the days my friends, we thought they would never end
Time and tide are never on our side
but as we are the heart of Wales, the land of song,
we must now bring our young folk on,
to try we must, to fail would be wrong,
we must, yes, we must fill that house with song.
There is something very special between
Wales and its people.
Let there be light and peace would be a bonus.

Susannah Burston

Love Slave

Your presence of being,
to me's - akin'ed in awe.
To the ultimate desire,
like the jewel of the Nile.
As both are solitary and singular
yet perfection's, one of a kind.

Just to be present in your radiance,
consumes me totally, heart and soul.
Love and lust indivisible,
as the two become one,
becoming the whole.

The need and yearning, from deep within,
my very existence, and flaming heart.
There is no wrong,
can be done - by you.

It's nothing this mere mortal soul,
could remove, destroy or reproduce.
So impossible for me,
after seeing your radiance.
And so with it, to embrace.

Yet! . . . When all of this,
is said and done.
My action's become,
and are singularly controlled.
As I'm a love slave, only to one.

So no matter what, tomorrow brings,
as always I'm yours,
to control - and yours,
alone to console.

Gary J Finlay

In Remembrance Of Cameron James Duffield 15th October 2004

Born still to this world you came our precious child,
A body so tender, your expression so mild,
Pure was your soul, innocent you were on Earth,
Your spirit, my child, has been given new birth,
No look of discomfort was upon your face,
Just a look of peace and heavenly grace,
Specially chosen you were by the Lord up above,
To sit by his side and surround us with love,
Yet from your sleeping body did your eternal spirit fly,
Touching our hearts and lives like an angel up on high,
It is sorrowful that we have had to part,
But forever and a day you shall remain in our heart.

Goodnight and God bless our child
Forever may you rest in peace.

Shadow Duffield

Advice

'Memories of him keep me going,' she says
Fondly remembering her lost mate.
I hear again how one should dwell
On little moments that were shared.

Too soon to recall shared moments,
That would give me pain.
'But it will ease,' she says
Fondly squeezing my arm again.

I nod agreement so she can leave
Not for me the endless talk.
I close my mind - appear unfeeling
Until my heart completes its healing.

June Kelsall

Remember That I Am Always Near

Don't ever forget that I am always near,
For I could never truly leave you, my dear,
This part of our journey has come to an end,
But please always feel the love that I send,
Our souls are entwined, never to part,
Eternally connected, heart to heart.

When you miss me whisper my name,
For I will surround you and ease your pain,
Feel my warmth, kisses and hugs,
Remember the good times and our love,
Hear my laughter filling each day,
And the good times we shared along the way.

Our love so precious and so strong,
With you my love I couldn't go wrong,
Remember our strength and the faith we shared,
The beautiful times when we hadn't a care,
We're together again when you think of me,
For I am living in your heart you see.

Sara Church

Dream Lover

The years roll by, but still it seems,
I have not yet realised my dreams.
I fancy through the night I see,
The one I love so close to me.
His arms around me doth entwine,
And for a while I call him mine.
But, with the dawn the dream departs,
Another day unsettled starts,
'Tis long but still I see it through,
To spend another night with you.

Agnes Driver

WIMPY LOVE

Back in the sixties, when skirts were skimpy,
We met after school and went for a *Wimpy.*
Your legs as we walked, such indelible charm,
As we went through the door; you on my arm.

With brain overheated - grabbing a table,
Wanting to speak but not being able,
Then, waiting for you to start the talk -
I tried to look nonchalant, spinning a fork.

The swing of your hair, the tilt of your head,
Your teeth as they bit into burger and bread.
The froth on our coffee, the coffee urn's shine,
The terrible glance of your eyes catching mine.
The far-reaching torrent of throbbing blood,
The rush in my head that my heart understood
And the certainty fate would take its course,
In the way that you passed the tomato sauce . . .

I heard that you married; it cut to the core,
Then, heard you divorced and got married once more.
But that's over as well; it all came to an end,
And you're just looking up a very old friend.

So, we're meeting again, forty years on,
Oh, how I regret that the *Wimpy* bar's gone,
And we may not have chance to relive that sweet link.
Now, where shall we meet? *McDonald's* I think.

Gol McAdam

EVERY TIME I . . .

Every time I see your face,
My mind starts to wander,
My heart starts to race.

Every time I hear you mutter,
Those three little words I long to hear you utter,

I love you

It's true I do, I love you,
I long to tell you but haven't the nerve to.

Will I ever have you? I guess only time will tell.
If only I could find a way, or that magic spell.

My dreams of you are heaven,
But the reality is just hell.

Will I ever get to hold you,
Or feel your warm embrace?

Who knows, but until that day,
Until I find that special place,

I guess I'll have to remain content,
Each time I look into your eyes,
And I gaze upon your face.

Robbie Shorey

Kiss

The dewdrop submits
its sloppy kiss
upon the rich morning.
The sunshine smacks
the sweet earth
as daylight is dawning.

A lover's kiss
awakens sleep
and stirs a warmth within
as they meet
strength swells
neither one giving in.

For some this is
the only way
that kisses
can be given
an act of intimacy
so much that
we have hidden
far from sight
and ridicule
judging it forbidden.

Kisses can mean
many things
hurt, love and farewell
truth it lies
far behind
the lips that cannot tell.

Sandra Roberts

Come Home Soon

You've gone away,
I miss you badly.
You are my world,
I love you madly.

Waiting, listening
For the phone to ring.
When it does,
My heart will sing.

In my sleep,
I reach for you,
Just empty space,
What will I do?

On my mind,
All the time.
This must be
How it feels to pine.

To hear your voice,
To feel your kiss,
To be in your arms,
Would be sheer bliss.

To have you back,
I'd pay a fee.
Whatever it costs
'Cos I love you Bre.

Gill Bestwick

Undying Love

You tell me that you love me, I wonder is it true?
You let me down in many ways, I do the same to you.
You tell me that you miss me when I'm absent, is it so?
When I phone and you're not there, my doubts begin to grow.
You tell me you get lonely, and you find that hard to bear.
Yet you don't have much to say to me, when I am with you there.
I worry sometimes, that you'll leave, it would be a bitter pill,
For even with my doubts and fears, I know I love you still.
And we still cling together, though the reasons are not clear.
Perhaps the thought of loneliness, could be our greatest fear.
I'm taking stock and thinking of the happy times we've shared
And I'm praying you'll remember, the way we two once cared.

Mary Goodchild

Mother And Son

I carried him around for months on end
I was only 18 but it was the trend
And then he arrived through sweat and tears
It would be hell on earth these next few years

Ten tiny fingers and ten tiny toes
Oh and that cute little button nose
Crying and demanding for that little white bottle
I remember thinking, I could easily throttle
And then through his school years
He brought me such joy
Oh how I loved my wee little boy

It starts again the circle of life
He's gone and got himself a wife
I'm on my own now, he's all grown up
I'm getting broody
I know, I'll buy a pup.

Marie Warrington

When Dame Fortune Smiled

(For Freda)

White hatted, neat in a pleated
Suit of blue, relaxing, she sits
Upon grass in Princes' Street gardens,
The cragginess of Edinburgh's castle
Softened by a touch of warm
Afternoon sun, and by the spontaneity
Of her smile, expressing a happiness
To treasure, a moment of real pleasure,
Fortuitously, forever preserved on film.

Clasped securely in her hand,
Scrolled inside its red boxed tube
Resides one of life's glittering prizes,
A university degree awarded with honours,
And which, on that special graduation day,
Was both a legacy of my industrious student
Past, and the key to an equally
Successful future career, and ambitions embracing
Hopes and dreams sufficient for two.

For almost from that one shared instant
In time, our disparate lives soon began
To intimately intertwine, to coalesce
Into an intense and loving wedded consummation,
And a life together which her hands
Helped fashion, using the same gentle
Sureness of touch once captured on camera,
When a heart was touched by a smile,
All those so very happy years before.

Andrew Farmer

WILL I LOVE AGAIN ANOTHER DAY?

What flows through this body of mine?
Is it true that love is totally blind?
A heartbeat, a blink of an eye,
Tears roll as I start to cry.

I was always there by your side,
Wept with you when you cried.
I never made promises I didn't keep,
Or said things to make you weep.

Is this a love I can never hold?
Will you always blow hot and cold?
Just when love I thought I had found,
You brushed me aside, crushed me to the ground.

You gave me the eye, then turned away.
To break my heart in every way,
Bittersweet you drove into my mind,
Leaving deep shadows of another kind.

Now you're gone, no more tears flow,
Nothing is left that I can show.
My soul, my spirit, taken away,
Will I ever love again, another day?

Alan J Morgan

ME

I look in the mirror and think *Oh Lord*
I am on that downward path
The wrinkles I see are mine all mine
A night out leaves an aftermath.
The sight's never pretty at this late age
But at least I am still here
In spite of having some bits removed
Oh dear! Pass another beer!
Of course I have memories to see me through
Of times when I was so slim
And all those boys who dated me then
All those Johns, Davids and Jim.
In those days all of our clothing matched
And heels were three inches high
Our gloves were of kid or maybe silk
And skirts *did* cover each thigh.
Those hats we wore, cocked over one eye
Made us look jaunty, but neat.
And those were the days when 'happy' was 'gay'
And afternoon tea was a treat.
I look in the mirror and think *so what*
My life's been quite good you see
I may not be young and surely not slim
But wrinkles and all it's still 'me'.

Elsie Sharman

Her Beauty Is Her Nature

I fondly remember the day we met,
and the times that we spent together.

From my birthplace in Wales,
motorcycling days, mountain walks,
viewing the splendour of the heather.

We camped below Harlech Castle,
as our ancestors doubtless did before
and other places such as this.

When Australia beckoned us to its warm climate,
we realised it would be such places,
that we will surely miss.

Adelaide became our home now,
it was Don Dunstans vision that we shared.

She made a perfect home for us,
we became a couple,
that's all we ever wanted or cared.

She learnt to cook and garden,
her passion for things new had no bounds.

The unfamiliar animals, birds and plants,
she absorbed with delight from our new surrounds.

Her zest for travel far and wide
in Australia was matched only by mine.

We shared such amazing sights and experiences,
that can only be described as divine.

From Cape York to Tasmania,
our camper van traversed this great land.

She was the perfect travelling companion,
I will always cherish the day she gave me her hand.

Our beautiful daughter was born,
we could deny ourselves a family no longer.

So a full-time mother she became,
a natural, a born to be, our love became stronger.

Alas today she is no longer with me,
the dreams we shared I can no longer fulfil.

But all those memories will never be forgotten,
of years ago, she is in my heart still.

Phil Albert Jones

LOST LOVE

Love breaks my back like it was a stick
Life crumbles its dried out clay
Dissect the faults, slowly I pick
Will I ever want to live, see another day?
Feelings take me back to how I felt
Memories play images inside my head
Ice feelings now will never melt
I remember the words you said
'I love you'
Ha! If only it was true
My mind, my body will deteriorate
Destroyed from within
Love could never even contemplate
Where life and love begin
You, I still need here
Please hear my words and lines
I am nothing to fear
I have told you that so many times
My life has only one concern
Will you ever return?

Richard Marshall-Lanes

Scantily-Clad Moment

For one second
you looked at me
and took from me
a shred of hope
that fed the fire
deep in your soul.
A second more and
you had enough
cupped in your hands
to pack the cracks
around your heart
for an eternity.
I opened my mouth
to swallow your smile
and let your lips
mutter and flutter awhile.
The empty spaces
at the centre of me
so quickly filled with
urgent kisses and
fabulous schemes,
to swell me and
grow me and feed me
on the echo of
half-formed promises
and erotic dreams.
We didn't speak,
but our fingers met
in brief caress and
understood without a word
that nothing more would
come of this.

The formal exchange -
coins, tickets and nods.
A moment had gone
and the bus rolled on.

Tina Bass

THE BEAUTIFUL ROSE

(For my sister Denise)

There was a flower, a beautiful rose
It bloomed through the years
But it faded away and bloomed no more
And left a garden full of tears.

Somewhere in another place
The rose still grows, is in full bloom
It's vibrant and as strong as ever
Just growing in another room.

You cannot see the rose no more
But you can feel it all around
It comforts and it speaks to you
Although you hear no sound.

Where it grows is a better place
It's happy and it's free
Swaying gently in the breeze
Its glowing beauty for all to see.

Donna Munson

PADDY

The alcoholic bundle slept beneath the stars,
Hoar frost the mucky mac adorned,
No Goliath frame all Trojan heart solid rock,
Brass bowelled, Paddy, breakfasts on steak and eggs all raw,
Raw as yesterday, fresh from the bullock's arse.

Sober on an empty pocket,
Belly growling, early hour,
Knock and chop, half an acre,
Stand at seven by George's door.
Knocking softly, hail to Mary,
Praying he will sub a draw.

Fags and grub at Little Cyril's,
School kids chase for far flung coppers,
Skin stained of soil,
A generous heart, God alone his better man
Scratta green or scratta white
His woodland home fair wind or foul.

One dozen bottled Guinness stock
The mucky mac his pantry
Old hedgehog's blanket, soft as down,
Cradles, 'Good luck' lad till dawn.

Les Dernie

My Photograph

I gaze into my photograph,
And thinking back I have a laugh,
At things I've said and done,
All because I was so young.

The fun I've had in the war days,
I never shall forget,
Suddenly, I say, 'Was that really me?'
As I'm gazing at myself.

I was so happy and carefree,
Nothing worried me,
And how I loved to dance.

Love in my day was innocent,
Not as it is today,
I went out with many a stranger,
But, they didn't have their way.

Now I am much older,
Though my hair is not all grey,
I do have some wrinkles in my face today.

And a poet I've become,
I'm still looking at my picture
Wishing I were still young.

D Petherick Cox

OPEN DOOR

The door was always open in Granny's wee house,
kettle forever on the boil, a mug of tea for all.

No riches or wealth did she have, but love she had in plenty.

One of God's angels she was, a kiss and cuddle when
ailing. A hand of firmness when bad.

Stories of days gone by she told when I was just a boy.

The smile on her face belied the hardship and
sorrow she had faced in life.

Children to her were gifts from God, she guarded
each with a passion. Equal share of her love she gave.

Now she tends to God's wee angels in Heaven above.

We miss and love you Granny.

God bless.

Norman Andrew Downie

DRESSED IN MOONLIGHT

I would come to you in evening,
My love alight, tremulous
Under midnight's carousel of stars.
Eager, in alabaster innocence,
To sip the cup of passion's longing -
To stand before you
Dressed only in a moonbeam's
Shimmering caress.

Lorraine Sautner

LOVE FOOLS

The day I believed I knew it all
Was my hardest drop, my highest fall.
A deplorable sense of sickness and doubt.
The realisation I'm not with, I'm without.

Stupidly clinging to strands of fresh air.
Another temptation, you joke - that's unfair.
The mountainous landslide broke who I was,
Now lost in the darkness, you fooled me because?

I swallow embarrassment, claw back my words.
Self will delivered just what I deserved.
Now back in the shadows, it's where I belong,
Thought it was meant to be, my thought was wrong.

J E Kirkman

DANCING DREAM

Just watched Come Dancing on TV
And for a little while
I'd love to be amongst them all
And wear my painted smile
To dance the tango
Maybe do the jive
Whiz around the floor with verve
What a gas -
At 75!
Well I can dream can't I?
I'd really enjoy it all
Next day I'd ache everywhere -
And just about manage to crawl!

Barbara Buckley

CONFESSION

Cornered between
A rock and a hard place,
Thinking of you
On St Valentine's Day.

Wanting to say
How much I'm besotted,
'Specially now
On St Valentine's Day.

And surely it's almost
Criminal not to
Talk of love
On Valentine's Day?

Really must curb
Intentions like these though -
You've turned me down,
So there I should leave it:

Mustn't destroy
Our *marvellous* friendship
By waiting and hoping
On Valentine's Day.

Thinking of you -
Not sure what to do -
Don't be offended -
It's Valentine's Day!

Wilson James

Just For Me

I think of you in name
My memories hold you close
God took you from this world
Just when you mattered most

I never thought I'd love again
The hurt was far too deep
Every day I think of you
Even see you when I sleep

I listened to your words
Please don't be alone
Just think of me now and then
As our memories grow old

Carry on regardless
I can no longer keep you safe
The love that we both had
No one can ever forsake

Never feel guilty
Don't think you've let me down
I want you to be happy
In someone else's arms

It's because I loved you darling
Please do this just for me
Make sure that when you love again
Your heart will feel free.

Lynne Taylor

HEART'S SONG

Since so few could play with me in the madness of this place
I picked up a pen and thought I might amuse myself by
telling a few tales . . .
I created a character, whom I called 'myself,' with perimeter
and bounds which I could not go beyond . . .
Then I found others who delighted in my game -
so much so that they gave it a name
The game they said should be called *life*, in it every person would
play a special part, they would love and wound, create both pleasure
and pain for all the other persons in this game . . .
And then by some sheer stroke of luck some of these persons
might actually wake up!
Those that did would tell a story, which really is quite ordinary . . .
It seems fun they'd say to play this game, until you're worn out,
by the pleasure and the pain
It may be then, you'll realise - you never looked into another's eyes
Those eyes you see they were your own, you never were
away from home!
All names and forms they will dissolve
When the heart is known, the game is over
It is then *real life* begins . . .

Justin Manchester

A QUESTION OF LOVE

Do not roses neglected die
if unloved?
Does not the heart remain unfulfilled
if not romanced?
And without a tender kiss to warm the lips
will not the soul remain cold?

Ian Benjamin

My Special Friend

Today I lost a special friend,
Someone I loved so dear.
A friend who was never demanding,
But who I knew would always be there.
A friend who never saw faults in me,
Who accepted me as I am.
And a friend who always behaved to me,
As gentle as a lamb.
A friend who was forever faithful,
Loveable, loyal, and true,
And a friend who instinctively knew,
Whenever I was blue.
My friend has left a very big space,
And an ache within my heart.
And now it feels so strange to me,
For us to be apart.
For my friend's name was Sadie,
Not a two-legged, but four-legged friend,
Who stuck by me through thick and thin,
Until the very end.
For a more loyal friend we will never find,
In our pets, be they big or small,
For an undying devotion and love,
Is what they give to us all.
So take good care of your special friend,
And enjoy them while you may.
For they leave a space nothing else can fill,
Every single day.

Caryn Smith

TRULY, HONESTLY, DEEPLY

Truly, honestly, deeply, I'm in love with you,
Forever always love I needed, you were there, and I succeeded.
When you leave me, I cannot go on,
Time stands still until I find a song.

A song that will stand the test of time, a song you will sing
and I know you are mine.
My heart climbs high and I leave it there . . .
I open my eyes and then I despair . . .
Cos you're not there.

My voice was lost amongst heartbreak and pain,
My smile it was false, gave others gain.
I tried and tried but loneliness came,
I could stand it no longer . . . you were not to blame.
It was so easy, sleep crept in, I let go, and my life had been, but . . .

Truly, honestly, deeply, I'm in love with you,
I stay with you each day and night,
And this time I take on the fight . . .
Guiding and guarding your every move, to keep you safe
until your life is through.
Until the day you come back to me, where we will be together,
Forever in eternity.

Janey French

BIRTHDAY BOY

I admire you
For the things you do,
You make us look unfit,
Don't get tired a bit,
Build house after house,
Scuttle about like a mouse
London to Scotland and back again,
In sun, hail, snow and rain,
Over your shoulder your camera will abide,
Everywhere you go, it doesn't leave your side.

Your surprise parties go down well,
When they're going to happen, no one can tell,
No bum fluff on the glasses,
He shouts to certain young lasses.

Your hats are great, they're really smart,
In fact you could say they're a work of art,
You kill every squirrel and cat you meet.
But I myself think they're kind of sweet,
Garlic over pizza that's the way,
But never enough for Uncle Ray,
What age you are it's not quite clear,
But happy birthday to you until next year!

Rebecca Muir (15)

LET ME LOVE YOU LOVE

Love what makes the world go round
And you're the finest one I've found
Let me hold you close
Let me love you just a little.

The moon has gone behind the cloud
And I wouldn't whisper very loud
Let me hold you close
Tell me you love me just a little.

Some folks talk about romancing
And say we shouldn't do it
Don't pay no attention to them
Because they didn't do it.

Just because the moon is bright
Then you know he's watching tonight
Let me hold you tightly
Let me love you again.

Just because it's dark out there
We can't see what we have to share
Let me tell you true
Let me whisper I love you.

R Duncan

LOVE SO FINE

A day dreaming
Sun slowly
Rising
Love so fine
Lips desire
A soft embrace.
True love
Beaming
Love me long.
A day dreaming
Moon slowly
Rising.
Deep in the night
Hearts beating
Laughing girls
Hearts awaken.
Love so fine
Deep in the night
Laughing girls
Are taken
Night falling
Love gently calling.

Geoff Carnall

The Spark

The exotic caress of love
Flicks its tongue behind your ear.
It wanders fleetingly
Down the line of your dress,
Shocking you with its tenderness.

You thought that you had forgotten
About love,

A sweet but distant memory.

Maybe you even forgot
That you were a woman.
Besieged by soaps
And lonely walks around the park.

Yet it only takes a certain smile.
Like a message in a bottle,
Sent first class, to re-ignite the spark.

David McConville

Red Poppy

This delicate ephemeron
shouts for joy
as it squeezes life between black asphalt path and
white-washed stonewall.
Such optimism humbles me
as I contemplate life
in the comfort of my seaside home.

Rose Lewis

YOU ARE NOT THERE

In my mind's eye I see you
as plain as day,
I smell your essence filling the room,
I sense your presence, in my solitude,
I hear your footsteps beside me,
I turn to face you,
but you are not there.

I hear your voice calling me,
your words are soft for me and me alone,
I see your face beckoning me,
a gentle smile on your lips,
I sense you touching me
but I feel nothing,
I turn to face you
but you are not there.

You were my lifelong companion,
my soulmate, my friend,
you were my sanity, my guide,
my mentor, my confident,
but where you are now?
I turn to face you
but you are not there.

Angie Edmonds

SPIRIT FREE

You make me feel alive inside
even though you are far away
you set my spirit free
bringing happiness to me

My eyes want to see you
feast upon your looks
I want to hear the sound
of your voice
will it turn me on so much?

I want to get up close to you
take deep breaths through my nose
smell the scent of your skin
oozing through your clothes

My lips want to kiss you
my tongue wants to tease yours
my arms want to hold you
wrap my love around you

I can't explain
the way you make me feel
my heart, body and soul craves
for your warm tender loving touch
if I was granted one single wish
I would wish that we were together
to spend a lifetime by your side
for this is my one true wish
you are a gift
my one and only
treasure.

Janet Topham

POLITE SOCIETY

'Mademoiselle you are attractive,
And sometimes you are exciting,
I duly accept your invitation,
So pleasurably and exacting,

With a message of love from far up above,
You entertain me gloriously within polite society,
So impeccable and impressive,
Where the night-time wind is furious and un-abating,

As love blossoms on your red lips,
I am moved with romanticism and hope,
You have seen and read my love letters,
Where the tempest stars shine magnificently above,

To elope with you Madame would be a dream,
Oh yes a simple dream put so innocently,
From within my tortured heart,
I am chained to destiny with fury,

Where the waves upon the mighty ocean crash,
Besides a desolate shore, I am subdued to fancy,
Underneath the bright crimson sky,
Whilst dreaming of sweet nothings,

The poetry book that I hold, is substantial,
It keeps me from going mad with despair,
Where the gods weep uncontrollably,
Where time and space has no meaning or reason,

My declaration is with fond sweet memories,
Of an endearing goddess of beauty strong,
With duplicity of your virtues,
I am caught like a wild hare,

Where Rome knows no weakness of character,
Only freedom and liberty to love you,
Is my guiding motto mademoiselle.'

James Stephen Cameron

All Or Nothing

She has a path to choose,
Her time is running out,
There is no win or lose,
In roads so full of doubt.

She knows the path of true,
Is the road that leads to you,
She fears she'll start and find you gone,
Left upon a road going on and on.

And the last grain now does fall,
Of times sands of mistakes,
This is it, she hears that call,
And now she has a choice to make.

For she has a road to choose,
Her time now is no more,
A love she has to lose,
Through a one-time opened door.

Two roads of choice she threw aside,
As a third from naught appeared,
Leading to the vast outside,
To all her deepest fears.

So there she goes round twists and turns,
Up hills and down, through ice and burns,
She's started now, no turning back,
It's all or nothing on love's unknown track.

Sarah Heptinstall

Guess Who?

She is beautiful!
Her skin is so soft - a little wrinkled, of course -
But still soft to the touch.
Her hair, snow-white, is the prettiest I have seen,
It too is silky and has an almost iridescent sheen.
Little tendrils of pure white curl around her head,
And laughing eyes of blue shine out their love.

She is kind!
Not just in the ways of generosity, many though they are,
But she lets one talk, tell her their troubles,
Listens with patience and understanding,
For she has seen many troubles of her own
And life is no closed book to her.

She is plump!
Oh, she won't mind me saying that.
Because she knows it's true and she's a very honest person.
In any case, I wouldn't have her any other way.
If she were thin, she would be gaunt and hard,
But she is soft, warm and cuddly.

She is young!
Oh you may laugh at that!
To look at her you may not think so,
But her mind is always running ahead,
On the alert, interested and interesting,
Keeping her young in thought and feeling.
And I love her so very dearly,
My aunt of eighty years!

Jean Ward

The Maid From The Sea

I saw your face in a haze of light,
My heart in ecstasy took flight.
There you stood on the shifting sand,
And I reached out to hold your hand.

A motionless host in the twilight,
A nimbus shimmering by night,
Your eyes aglow like the flaming fire,
To set my heart ablaze with desire.

I held your hand on that golden beach,
The careless joy of love to reach,
Beside the waves we laughed and ran,
Playing as only lovers can.

But come the morning you had flown,
Once more I wandered all alone,
You'd gone to where you were always free -
A thousand leagues beneath the sea!

Mary Baird Hammond

By Way Of Thanks

(For Connor)

I see the reflections
I feel Your embrace
I see how Your Love shines down on His face.

The way He smiles
The way He laughs
The way His eyes do shine

I know He is for all the world
But You,
You made Him Mine.

April Dickinson-Owen

The Golden Room

A very special room
On a very special day
Awaited our arrival
As we made our way.

All was set in the sunshine
Welcoming us glowing bright
Smiling faces greeted us
Filling us both with delight.

Places set on a golden cloth
A candle surrounded by flowers
Ready for all to dine
For many happy hours.

A beautiful cake in the window
Said 'Happy 50th Anniversary'
With bouquets of lovely flowers
For everyone to see.

A sparkly, framed picture of us
On our wedding day
A golden 50 beside it
Was there on display.

'Happy Golden Anniversary'
Was shining everywhere
As we dined together
Enjoying all the fare.

Kind words were spoken
With many a fond embrace
How happy we all were
In that golden place.

Barbara Fosh

Matthew

When the new shoots come
And the blades grow green;
When the new buds show
In the springtime sheen;
When the soft rain falls
On the open earth,
Then I'll look in hope
For your own re-birth.
I'll know you're there
And I'll hear you say,
'I'm beside you now
We'll meet one day.
You gave me all
And I love you so;
I don't know why,
But I had to go.
I know you hurt
In my sorrow's act.
I was lent, not given.
That wasn't the pact.
Try to remember
The times we had,
And think of me now,
No longer sad.'
Oh yes, I'll remember,
But tears must fall,
For we love you, Matthew,
We love you, all.

Elizabeth Morris

LOVE THROUGH THE YEARS

Through childhood days
In many ways
We've grown so close together,
In times of trial, sometimes denial
No matter what the weather.

I never said too much back then
But words
were hard to find,
I only knew I couldn't leave
A chance like this behind.

You never knew
How I felt about you
I kept it all inside,
Perhaps it was your tender age
Or just my stubborn pride?

From day-to-day as time went on
My love grew ever fonder,
Through aching heart
And years apart
I wondered how much longer?

Then came the day I had to lave
And bid my friends goodbye
With one last glance
I'd missed my chance
My heart began to die.

John H Foley

UNTITLED

(Written for my eldest brother, David
who died from sclerosis of the liver, aged 32)

I've sat all week
And racked my brain,
Asking why?
My heart in pain.

This was not fair
Of one so young
For Mam and Dad
To lose their son.

For Sharon and Gary
Their heads all a mess
Now that they have
One brother less.

For the rest of the family
Who are sat here today
Helping us through
To show us the way.

To all of his friends
Whose hearts must be aching
I'll tell you this
Mine is just breaking.

For the loss of my brother
Is too hard to bear
When he called out my name
I was not there.

I'm here for my family
Through thick and through thin
But we'll keep asking ourselves
God, why was it him?

We'll I'll finish my poem
I have no more to say
God bless you Dai
You're now on your way.

On your final journey
To who knows where
With God beside you
To show you He cares.

Goodnight David, God bless.

Vivienne John

REGENERATION

The wheels are idle,
Everything has stopped,
Just the indistinct creaking, groaning aloft.
Work has ceased for evermore,
The end of an era for them all,
No son to follow father's footsteps,
No tales to tell when deep below,
Its wheel has stopped forever more.
No air; no life,
Just dereliction.
Clearance begins,
Plumes of dust begin to fly,
Settling thick upon the floor,
Covering the site,
The community is done,
Ended as if with a single shot,
From a gun;
Regeneration - what is it all for?

Wendy Brittain

TRUE LOVE

(Written for Jay)

The thoughts of your smile, of your tender touch,
Bring warmth and wanting, I miss you so much.
I long for the moment when your lips touch mine,
I yearn for you to hold me, for our souls to entwine.
Each day my love grows stronger, each time I think of you,
My heart is filled with immense love, it helps to get me through,
Through the moments of uncertainty, when I ache to hold you near,
The thoughts of what we have and share erases all the fear.
I close my eyes and you are there forever in my heart,
And though there may be distance, we'll never be apart,
I want to show you every day how much you mean to me,
And let you know for you my love is for eternity.

N Roberts

THIS ONE SECRET

I want to tell you
Please let me tell you
I don't care you may see me a silly
I don't care you will find me a fool
For all the secrets we have shared
This one I have kept long enough from you
I ask my soul
I search my heart
I know a piece of it has already been lost for good
I may be a silly
And I don't mind being a fool
If this is all it costs me
To have you stop and listen
A woman to her man
When I tell you, 'I love you.'

Cherub Tang

The Promise

You once gave me a promise,
That your love for me was long.
But that promise that you gave me,
How it turned out wrong.
You once gave me a promise,
That your love for me was true.
But that promise that you gave me,
Was false and well you knew.
You once gave me a promise,
That your love would never die.
But that promise that you gave me,
Was turned into a lie.
You once gave me a promise,
That your love would never end.
But that promise that you gave me,
Was broke and will not mend.

Sue Brown

To My Granddaughter

Alison - oh! rose of mine,
Sweetest darling child.
Sunny smile and hair so fine -
    And gold as sand.

The early morning dew is fresh -
Upon her face so fair.
And in her merry dark eyes
    Moonbeams dancing.

Run and play and laugh and sing -
Ring a ring o' roses,
A perfect little girl is she
    Alison Victoria!

Ellen M Lock

GOODNIGHT GRANDAD . . . SWEET DREAMS

(In memory of James D Webster, passed away 23/09/1985)

I once knew a dear and special man
My grandad was his name
But he was taken away - and I've not seen him -
Since the day the angels came.

They took him up to Heaven
To dwell with God above
To cure him of his ailments
And live in a world of eternal peace and love.

It broke my heart to lose him
It's ached since the very day he died
I'd never felt such pain before
Nor cried, just quite how I have cried.

But I still hold his loving memory
And in my heart that will remain forever dear
For no matter whatever the distance between us
I know our souls will always be so near!

Louise Pamela Webster

THE LAST TIME WE WERE FRIENDS

(For my friend Michelle. You'll always be my friend)

Little did we know that our adventure to Spain
Would be our very last, together, as best friends.
We set off in the coach and travelled many miles;
Excitedly gossiping, not being able to hide our smiles.
Eventually we reached the place - Barcelona our destination
And settled into the hotel with very little hesitation.
Then we went out drinking with some teachers there
And some got drunk, singing karaoke
Which is just what we had feared!
We saw many grand sights and lazed on a white sand beach,
Drunk loads of Vodka; maybe a glass too much each!
Remember going back, trying to unlock the door?
Even the youngsters saw us falling laughing on the floor!
Yet this came to an end and unknowingly our friendship too,
I don't really know what happened and doubt neither do you.
But now time has passed, I look back with a massive smile,
We thought friendships lasted forever but we were just both in denial.
But just when we finished, as our friendship ends,
Just remember we had a great time,
The last time we were friends.

Nykki Welcomme

YOUR FACE AND THE ROSES

I touched the roses this morning
And they smiled at me softly
I touched them once, twice and oh it felt so velvety
I smelt them and its scent was as sweet as the heavens
I turned to take my leave, but I could not resist its beauty
It smiled at me again, I looked closer
And I saw a face . . . the face . . .
The face of beauty
It was serene
I saw a hand . . . a hand on the rose
I touched it
I smelt its perfume and oh, I reminisced
I saw your face on the roses
The face of love, the face of beauty
The face of friendship, the face of the morrow
I saw your face on the roses like never before

Joseph Iregbu

UNTITLED

I tremble at the thought of her,
Sweet fragrance overwhelming,
Complexion to humble porcelain,
A smile of prayers answering.

To hold so close and feel the warmth,
As her body permeates my heart,
Careful in case she should break,
In my arms to stay, never part.

So grateful for my eyes,
This vision forever a part of me,
To behold until time is spent,
Lest her beauty ever set me free.

Ken Clayton

Maid Of Paradise

We shall meet in cool and torchlit courtyards,
the silent precincts of night's sweet embrace
and bathe there in gentle fountains, where clear
sparkling waters cleanse past's tainted trace.
A couch waits, draped with fine silks and linens,
dates and almonds rest upon a silver tray,
before us a feast of new beginnings,
each choice placed like a jewel in the display.

Scents of jasmine and musk intoxicate us,
the stars anoint the bed where we will lie.
Your eyes are like the gates of seven heavens,
four basilisks stand ready to defy
mortality - and all time's hungry hunters
who would pursue us to this den of peace;
bring their pious rules here to confront us
and spoil the pleasure we have in our feast.

Your body like a slice of moonlight
falls softly on this torn and battered frame,
opens to me and lets our beings unite
to best the gods at their fate, their chosen game.
The gentle night will hide and protect you
but when cruel dawn calls, bidding you depart
I will beg Cronos halt the sun and let you
forever be the houri of my heart.

Note: The houri, in middle eastern mythology are Maids of Paradise, the virgins who will serve the faithful in the afterlife.

Ian R Thorpe

Guardian Angel

You look down on me from above with your tender care and
endless love.
By my side, away from harm, you are always there to keep me calm.
When I shut my weary eyes and pray, there you are for me each day.
Your love is endless and in my despair, guardian angel I know you care.
Take pity on me and see me right, with all your wisdom, all your might.
Wipe my tears, those painful years, guide me forward the angel
of the Lord.
You showed me the light to do the things I can, and without you
angel, I would not be the person I am.
My shining light, and my loving guide, you showed me the way
to help me right.

Mahala Tomaszko

Loved And Lost

Days of long lasting love,
Wasted on fags and beer,
The more I think of it,
No more do I want to hear,
I now know why our love couldn't last,
No more do I want to live in the past,
The way your lips felt on our first kiss,
From our first glance I never made you a miss,
I don't get why I was so misunderstood,
You were never there,
You were off with that s**t,
Was it love
Or just a sham?
You were treating me,
As bad as she,
Our marriage was not meant to be.

Vikki-Leanne Wood

I Wish . . .

The mist lifts
The silhouettes of humans appear
As they make their way about their business.
'Click!'
The door closes.
I see him striding down the path
Briefcase in his hand.
He opens the car door
Starts the engine and drives away.
I wave goodbye.
The monochromatic view of the world
Disappears as the sun rises.
I drop the curtain
And close my eyes.
I wish . . .

Melinda Penman

Katie

My Katie, I feel so blue
life is so lonely without you.
I miss your cuddles, love and care.
I look for you but you're not there.
Darling Kate, how could I let you go?
Dear Lord, I don't think I'll ever know.
My heart is broken, I feel bereft,
constant heartache since you left.
If only I could turn back time,
my darling Katie you'd still be mine.
I know I'd never let you go,
my Katie, I truly love you so.

Irene Keeling

LOVE THAT I LOST

I wake up in the morning and all is dark,
The heavy rainclouds surround my heart.
Love has been lost in hills that surround,
I will go searching, in hope to be found.
From day to day I aimlessly wander,
How to fix what is broken I ponder.
There is only one remedy, I begin to believe,
The love of my woman is all to relieve.
But how can I regain the love I have lost,
Not realising how much my actions would cost?
Never again will I be such a fool,
Not showing my feelings and acting so cool.
I'll be a new man, wear my heart on my sleeve,
Be honest and true and never deceive.
Take care of the woman that I love so dear,
The one that I need, that I have to be near,
Show her that I understand my mistakes,
I'll be sorry for everything, whatever it takes.
I'll promise that she can trust me so,
Make it clear that it is her that I owe,
My effort, honesty and what matters most,
To never, ever, burn her toast!

Richard J Smith

THE QUANDARY OF 'LOVE'

If it is 'love' that is the answer to all of men's trivial ills
Then why is it that only women are gifted with 'love's' skills?
For men can waste a lifetime just trying to understand
Just why the weaker women always have the upper hand

For century upon century women's dominance has prevailed
Whilst every attempt by men to rule has always badly failed
For women's tricks and wicked wiles have always won the day
So, how are men fooled into thinking they have the final say?

For 'love' can strike a man when he's not quite fully prepared
It is the sort of thing that happens and leaves them very scared
But women know the answers, how to claim 'love's' costly gains
Leaving men to wonder why they've been hit by 'love's' bitter pains

Is it men's physical make-up which leaves men so easy to tease
Or can it be true that women are only trying their men to please?
Perhaps their men are easily caught in the women's well-laid plans
By visions of 'love' that activates and violently affects their glands

The physical side of women must be the answer to make 'love' just
Or is it the simple answer that men can only think in terms of 'lust'?
Two four-letter words that sum up clearly the quandary of 'love'
Cheer up men and quietly accept if you must have 'lust' call it 'love'.

Brian Taylor

War - Is It Pointless?

War is stupid, war is our foe,
And still into battle, the soldiers must go.
The question is plainly, what for?
Why must guns fire and why must blood pour?
The answer is simple, because of Man's greed,
Because we think everything is what we need.
So for land and money, thousands must die,
Under a once peaceful, now bloodstained sky!
'Over the top!' the general calls,
He climbs, runs, shoots, and then he falls.
Besides his friends, he draws a breath,
And shuts his eyes for a well-earned rest.
He was one of many who died for us,
As a result of Man's greed and also because,
Man will never stop, won't learn from mistakes,
Will keep on wanting more no matter how high the stakes.

Emmeline Michelle Cambridge

Just As You Think . . .

Just as you think
You know all about yourself
You change
Your world is rearranged
Just as you think
You could never love again
Your heart is swept off to a new domain
Just as you think
You have everything in control
Your mind is not whole
Blinded by confusion
Delirious delusion

Mandy Thomas

ROMANCE

A long time ago you asked me to dance
and this was the start of a long romance.
Before too long we were planning our life,
for you had asked me to be your wife.
It was easy to answer as we both felt the same,
we loved each other right from the heart.
So hand in hand as we walk each day,
we pay no attention to the people who look at the old couple
who pass them by.
Still in love with a glint in their eye.
Time has tried the years have tested and together we still walk
hand in hand
Caring, sharing and loving each other,
that something special we knew would last.

Jean Adam

MY FIRST SONNET

(Dedicated to 'handsome')

Somewhere amongst the darkest of deep skies
Swims my past. Swims my fears. Swims destiny
Seek me and thou shall find no more lies
My destiny so bright it overpowers me
My love for you drowning in hate and bad
My soul standing proud and ever so tall
Your tears saving me from all that made sad
You must catch me from this lasting freefall
Open your arms my one truest love please
See the path I'm walking to our paradise
Bleed the blood from your heart to your knees
I can pay you the meaning of love's price
Given the chance when you decide to open
I will love you till no more words are spoken

Claire Valentine

A Proper Dinner

Yes, I know that 'dinner' is not the correct term for 'lunch'.

It's just what we used to say - let's see if we can go to Mum and Dad's
on Sunday 'for a proper dinner'.

Sunday lunch was always fun with Mum and Dad.
We'd have a few sweet sherries in those tiny ruby red glasses.
Well, Mum and I would, Dad used to have just a small one
and made it last.

There would often be a beef joint - sirloin or topside -
roasted to extinction and carved very thinly
making the delicate tracery of each slice just melt on the tongue.

A modest joint goes a long way this way - away into the future of
my memory in fact as I recall its silkiness and flavour now today.

It was served with cauliflower cheese, Yorkshire pudding with
onion gravy, and big brown roast potatoes - you remember -
all crisply toasted and cooked directly in the fat from the joint,
in the days before cholesterol consternation.

My own are but a pale imitation, sprayed with a mist of extra virgin
olive oil for the sake of health and not enjoyment and roasted
in the hope of producing something approaching Mother's
but failing every time.

Nowadays, I try to replicate this Sunday luncheon as often as possible
but it must have been a question of time
that made Mum's proper dinner such a pleasure -
she never seemed rushed in preparing it and we always
enjoyed the family camaraderie of washing up together afterwards,
whereas now I flop exhausted into the nearest armchair
when the meal is over and hope that someone will relieve me
of the need to clear away and load the dishwasher.

A country childhood, fresh garden produce and leisurely meals
always taken together - my parents' unique gift to me,
though sadly one I am unable to pass on.

Since their time, our age has moved into another century
with its own velocity and equally fast food.

I raise my imaginary glass of Dad's parsnip wine
in memory of 'a proper dinner'!

Maureen Horne

QUIVER

She cowers in the kitchen just sitting by the door
Her whole body is a quivering
She just couldn't take no more.

His fists rain down upon her
He's beating her black and blue
One question remains unanswered
Whatever did she do?

Did she deserve to live in pain and fear?
All she could do was shed a tear
She begged him to stop as he pulled her by the hair
He didn't have a heart, he just didn't care.

One day she will go travelling
Across the deep blue sea
Her fears will be no more as they will be set free
No more tears will she cry
Only smiles you will see.

Michelle Hinton

GOING FIRST . . .

Remember me when you grow old
Recall my smile and nerve so bold
Don't forget my love and passion
Nor my style and lack of fashion

Look at scenes of times gone by
Funny haircuts and me so shy
Times of innocence, hope and joy
Love at first sight, girl meets boy

Live again our days together
Summer nights and stormy weather
Hours of picnics, meals and talking
Sunny beaches, seagulls squawking

Hear once more our children's laughter
Tales of happy ever after
Tears of joy and tears of sorrow
Striving hard for their tomorrow

If I could have our time again
It would, of course, be just the same
Goodbye sweet love, my heart is breaking
Forget me not but keep on living

I will stay with you all your days
Helping you through in many ways
Until our paths cross one more time
Then you will be forever mine

Sam Kelly

POORLY WOLF

I sit here in the dark and shed my silent tears,
I'm waiting for an angel to wash away my fears.

I'm blinded of the love around me,
It screams to be known.
Something is keeping it from me,
I beg my captors for it to be shown.

My hand is not its own,
It casts a shadow of a different shape.
The stealer of souls has taken myself,
I feel rotten, rancid, raped.

The wolf inside me has been taken ill.
He worries, whines, whimpers.
He needs his caring partner back.
It seems nothing could be simpler.

But his partner washes his war wounds,
In a puddle of sorrowful sands.
I can't escape the pain I feel,
Even if I travelled all lands.

My eyes are a mystery to me;
They leak translucent pearls of hurt,
They leave contrails laced with loss.
With a dagger of damnation I flirt.

My world consumed by misery,
Emptiness is queen.
I pray to higher powers,
To shield the world from what I've seen.

Cameron Wolf

THE FIRE'S GOLDEN LIGHT

Whispered words of love fall from his sweet lips
Darkness cloaks the room as hands rest on my hips
I feel a rain of kisses fall upon my face
As we are locked as one, in an everlasting embrace

The ticking seems to stop from the clock upon the wall
As in a fatal love, I unknowingly start to fall
As I look into his face I see his soul beneath his eyes
And the brightness of our love hides the pack of lies

We start to move together in the rhythm lovers know
Basking in the warmth from the fire's golden glow
I touch his face and hair as if to prove that he is real
As we take the ultimate chance upon the lover's wheel

To the peak of ecstasy we glide as one body and soul
Finally two searching halves becoming one exultant whole
And as the feeling hits we float up upon a cloud
Dropping the rules of earth like an unwanted shroud

When our passion is spent I lay across his skin
Feeling the heat of our love the joy starts seeping in
He looks into my eyes and softly strokes my hair
I feel I have found my soulmate within our lover's lair

He begins to move away from me and fear clutches my heart
I want to plead with him to stay but my stubborn lips will not part
He turns and look straight through me and says he has to leave tonight
But he will always remember me in the fire's golden light.

Janine Ayres

The Lonely Chair

Hovering around, the customers
viewed impatiently, tables empty for
their full-up trays and chose
wisely, those not near the door.

Likewise, I too sought my special
place, to consume the steaming coffee
frothed up, yet black as night,
matching the mood inside of me.

Once settled, my gaze flitted
over the chattering throng
but the lonely chair drew me close,
emotions in turmoil. Life gone wrong!

Its aura kept a silent vigil there.
Happy laughter had once filled
pervading air, reflecting past meetings.
Sadness emitting now, from that lonely chair.

I tried to wrench my gaze, to link
with other subject in that busy clatter,
but that lonely chair was magnet to my eyes
and ears were shut to all pervading chatter.

My heaving heart would not admit
even a feather lift to ease my gloom,
and sore I wished that I had never viewed,
that lonely chair within that room.

This self-inflicted pain I knew was wrong.
I should have shunned this place, should not be there,
where we had gorged our love and supped romance.
But now cruel Death had placed that lonely chair.

Aleene Hatchard

A Lesson In Love

I tried
Reasoning with your mind
Yet I found it so very hard.
I learnt
That playing with fire, I would get burnt
Leaving ashes of my broken heart.

I needed
Love from you and I pleaded
Until there were no more words to say.
I cried
Every single tear I had left inside
But you still walked away.

Goodbye
Ask yourself the reason why
You hurt the way you do.
Finally
After all this time I am truly happy.
I married someone I love.
    It wasn't you.

Louise Allen

Stuck In Love

My heart yearns for relief
From this pain centred.
My chest heaves with love and loss

Feelings build
Love hurts
Why?

Ali Newman

I Think We Need To Talk

I think we need to talk about who we really are.
About why we sit in silence as we travel in the car.

I think it's time to sit down for the hundredth bloody time.
Burst a few pink bubbles, fetch a shovel and some lime.

For there are many dead things stinking out this place.
Things that we should bury and things that we should face.

I don't think that I love you, and that's so hard to say.
I know you've seen this coming and have avoided this day.

Still, I think that we should talk before one of us dies.
Before we start to hate each other, before we both start telling lies.

Much damage has been done and I don't think we can mend.
As it's been such a long time since I saw you as a friend.

We live in different worlds, see things so differently.
You see a dreamy drifter; I feel you suffocating me.

So much has been taken for granted and no feelings thought about.
So I think we need to talk, finally sort this relationship out.

Annette Phillips

Untitled

For a moment close to you
I'd risk anything
For a touch of your hand
My heart'd sing
For a glimpse of the eyes
Of my gorgeous queen
I'd always be a king

Haitham Hafez

A Tribute To Princess Diana (Queen Of Hearts)

St James' Palace, where she lay, was visited both night and day
By thronging crowds who'd come to mourn, and waited there
from dusk to dawn
To sign their tributes in a book or come to take a closer look
At floral tributes placed on ground - perfuming air whilst all around
Shocked horror of just how she'd died had stirred a nation to her side
Just wanting to be near to grieve, nor really wanting to believe
A nation joined as ne'er before - had come to worship and adore
The memory of a young princess who'd often shown a humbleness
By holding hands of HIV - 'twas filmed for all the world to see
Whilst touching them and giving hug - could not inherit super bug
To ban landmines she fought a war - persuading countries to deplore
The aftermath of bitter strife - the wounded, maimed, the loss of life
Her memory will live on as saint - will never tarnish - never taint
Our Queen of Hearts - Princess of Wales - remembered as our
fairy tales

M M Roach

Cold Water

You taste
Like
Cold water
Better
To warm
My summer nights
Come softly
When I sink into your
Icy depths
And we'll surface
To a breath's rhythm

David Woods

First Kiss

I love you with all my heart
And have done so from the start
Finding you, oh, what bliss
Forever remembering our first kiss
I hope we will never part
If we did it would break my heart
For you give meaning to my life
And I long to be your wife
To share our love through the years
Filled with laughter, empty of tears
Having children, one by one
Perhaps a daughter first, then a son
If we're blessed with more than two
Then I know what we must do
Raise them all to be good and kind
And tolerant and loving to all mankind
Then when we are all alone
We'll still love each other like Darby and Joan
I'll thank the Lord I became your wife
And that you let me share your life.

Diana Daley

To My Dear Wife

Wishing you a very happy birthday
and hoping you live to see many more.

I love you just the same, dear
as when we first did meet
I shall love you to the end, dear,
and I shall kiss you on your cheek.

From your ever-loving husband.

Amy Barrett

FINALITY

The love that was growing, steadfastly glowing
Now barely showing, ebbing and slowing.
For all the good years.
Now bad feelings and fears.

She pleads, she denies.
There will be no goodbyes.
His eyes leering, his voice jeering.
Her eyes crying, her heart dying.

To make a stand a final demand
Her heart will break
Left alone with 'the ache'
Resolute in his word, only pain felt and heard.

He slams the door.
She falls to the floor
Once loved greatly, immensely, a lot
Now crushed and bereft and mainly forgot.
Left alone to face the pain and the reality
Summed up in one word, that being 'finality'.

Ellen Spiring

So Perfect

I thought I could never love again
But you came along and eased my pain

When I first saw you it was love at first sight
At last I had found my Mister Right

You were everything I wanted and more
I loved you the minute you walked through the door

I knew my search was over at last
And all my hurt was now in the past

I always believed you were heaven-sent
You made me see what true love meant

Your love means more than words can say
I love you more with each new day

I feel so lucky you came into my life
And feel so privileged to be your wife

There's someone for everyone, or so they say
I know I found my perfect love that day.

Pauline Mayoh-Wild

Washed Form In Moonlight

Washed form in moonlight beyond my reach
I can taste still your breath
Lingered in taste against my tongue
Natural, surrendered and stolen

Lustre silk spilt onto cloth
Forsaken, I absorb you
For just a moment
I come into your beauty

The stars in all the breadth of Heaven
Have arrived, their slight luminance now
Come stretched across ageless depth
To create a silver edge to your silhouette

Here in thunder's pause I sit
In wonder of this disclosure
So unworthy, so aware
So full of you

There is no reason here
You see in me
That completeness which I see in you
I am ashamed before your beauty

I beg the mercy of the moonlight
Adorned on your surrendered form

Terry L Cummings

Goodbye, Grandma

My grandma is fading; she's preparing to leave
Her body is failing, she struggles to breathe.
Her arms lie limp, wet rags by her side
And behind her great smiles; fears she tries hard to hide.
I don't want her to leave me; it's selfish I know,
I just need her with me; I don't want to go.
When she holds my hand, and whispers my name
My heart glows with pride, she rekindles the flame.
I don't know if she realises just how special are her smiles,
When she walks by my side, I could continue for miles.
She's always been so strong, and feisty, so loved,
I just hope when she's gone, they are grateful above.
She'll shine from the heavens, and sparkle in the stars,
I hope that she knows I'll always hold her tight in my heart.
I pray Lord, please adore her, as much as she deserves,
Because you'll have one more angel, no longer here on Earth.
And one more thing, while I'm talking, I need her to know,
How much I will miss her, and do love her so.
She's my grandma, my angel, and my true best friend,
My memory of her will never come to an end.
I love her with every grain of my soul,
Having her as my grandma is what helped make me whole.
So please hold her safely, for the time, when it's due,
That we'll be together again, I ask that of you.

Goodbye my angel.

Caroline Roe

Blinded By An Unseeing Heart

When unsighted from the time of birth,
    Born in conditions of the lowest worth,
The struggle for self is much harder still,
    A test of the heart, and mind, and will,
To seek a goal, that's unvisually seen,
    Takes great moral courage and self-esteem.

To meet the challenges of daily life,
    Aided by the love of his loyal wife,
Then children three, who did him fulfil,
    And in a father much pride instil,
The hazards of life he then had to face,
    No matter at what the speed or pace.

In rising up from the lowest grade,
    Great efforts at all stages he made,
Were it in trade union or in politics,
    He had to master all of the tricks,
When sight from first concept of life is lost,
    Success will come at a much higher cost.

Should he, in time, his first family lose,
    Another love his heart needs to choose,
One who will give him an affection true,
    Who in him will new faith imbue,
Then to that love his heart would give,
    Two lovers as one together to live.

When love runs strong, in body and mind,
    Other thoughts the senses often blind,
While he had not the good sense to see,
    His judgement would in great danger be,
In making a choice, or taking a chance,
    Once taken, it would not his life enhance.

Having taken the decision, then others did say,
Had things been done in some other way,
The decision taken would be unquestioned now,
Not just what he did, but also how,
When for a lover, good judgement he lacked,
Vetting papers which were then fast-tracked.

The lover he trusted has now turned her back,
When giving the facts she candour did lack,
To her lawful spouse she turned for support,
He, an innocent party, did then retort,
'Were she to die and be placed in a grave,
She'd want to know who beside her was laid.'

Belatedly now, his past life he ponders,
As lately to childhood places he wanders,
Looking back on his life with mixed emotions,
Reflecting again on his foolish notions,
He sacrificed all to become a new dad,
All for the boy he calls his 'little lad'.

Edward Williams

SAVE US ALL

God save us all from politicians,
Civil servants, statisticians.
All these people rule our days
In myriads of different ways.
All our earnings and our pensions
Are ravaged by their interventions.
Government at every level,
Seems to eagerly bedevil.
All attempts to put away,
Something for a rainy day.
'You've had so much,' they say -
Then promptly spirit some away.

Janet Cavill

Old Whitby

Set upon a rocky cliff
The ancient abbey stands
Perched like a sentry
On guard over the old town below
Well-worn steps lead down
To houses and shops
With red pantiled roofs
Huddled around the harbour
Where fishing boats unload their catches
Twin piers like crab's claws
Reach out into the sea
Reclining on a bench
The old fisherman
Cast upon the shore
Reflects on days past
When he would set sail with the fleet
To reap the harvest of the sea
Hauling in nets
Bursting with silver-skinned fish
Now he puffs contentedly
His mind filled with pipe dreams.

Terence Leslie

REFLECTING

As much as it's not
me who makes the light
embrace your face and
blow out like a fire
ball engulfing my
cornea, branding
my retina and
racing on my nerves -
petroleum streaks -
till it flares in my
head and sends heatwaves
through the dark densely
packed wet throb of life
inside these ribs of
mine, it is not me
who had a hand in
your radiant face.
But I melt muscles
expand pupils as
you see me seeing
you and we become
the heart of the sun.

Ryan Ormonde

My Parents

Well, Mum and Dad, what can I say
To you two, my parents, who made me this way?
When I look in my mirror I see you both there
Mum's shape of the face and Dad's bloody hair!
I carry you with me wherever I go,
The lessons you taught me I remember you know.
I know not to walk barefoot or smoke in the street,
To be nice and polite to the people I meet.
Those words of advice, well they came from Dad -
He had plenty of them and all drove me mad!
I sound more like you, Mother, day after day
When I'm nagging the kids to just go away.
If I have a complaint, it's one very small -
I wish you had made me just a little bit tall!
But I love you both dearly and I really am glad
That I managed to get me the best Mum and Dad.

Debbie Strange

Go Quickly

I thought I could not say goodbye
But it's harder still to watch love die.
So if your place is by her side
Then go, but let me keep my pride.

Go quickly, please don't stop to take
My hand, because my heart will break
Before you leave, and in my pain
I'll beg you to come back again.

Go quickly, don't look back to see
The way my tears are blinding me.
When my eyes are dry, when you are gone,
I'll start my life again, alone.

Tina Molli

SWEET SORROW

Seated on the platform bench
Hands clasped clinging together
Oblivious to others
Uncaring of the passing trains
We search each other's eyes.
For unspoken messages
With broken voices and
Faltering words we wait for
The train that will take you away
Hoping that it will be late
For you my love are leaving
Through necessity not choice
Leaving me here alone
And so for now we must part
Until at last we meet again
You go with my love and my heart

Terry Daley

DADDY'S DIY

Work, work, work,
That's all my dad ever does,
When he comes home from employment,
You would think he would come home for enjoyment!

Ivy Horner (10)

Angelic Affection

I looked through the east and I looked through the west;
Looking for someone not comparable with the rest.
I wondered if there were angels on this Earth!
Who could colour your life with love and mirth.
Millions of men I came across;
But found no one I could really applaud.
My search came to an end when I realised;
The angels I sought with me reside.
Sent for us, no doubt, God had;
Angels none other than my loving mom and dad.

Like a gardener nurtures the flower since seed;
Protecting them from every thorn and weed;
You took care of us with love and heed;
Fulfilling our each and every need.
You embellished us with fine education;
Civility and ethics are your donation.
What we are today is just because of you;
Count your favours, oh we can never do.
For all the things you have done so well;
You're a perfect match! One can tell.

I thank the Lord a whole lot;
Such blessed fortune upon me He brought;
Having you I am the richest;
Such Mom and Dad that are the best;
You are my most valuable possession;
My treasure is your care and compassion.
My deepest gratitude I wish you could see;
The more I thank you less it'll always be.
Successfully through life, may you take us ashore;
And we may live together for evermore!

Samreen Seher

EMBERS

In the flames
I watch desire grow

then flicker away

Sitting alone
beside this crumbling fireplace

something is missing

In the flames . . .

I see your spirit
                    dancing,
leaping, sparkling, wishing

owing nothing to eternity

My wondrous, fragile, pretty angel
soaring high upon your brittle sparrow's wings
absolving the world with your gracious rhythm
making this life one joyous hymn

until a sudden breath
takes you away
again

And my hurt lies
scorched

along a bleak horizon

nothingness, now in your place
reaching out, towards a photograph

my soul expiring

in the flames . . .

Steve Gunning

First Love

(For Horia)

Recording its presence, past leaves blanks, the way angels do.
You're beautiful even when you left, love letting loose its sides.

Your image, like my mother's tongue, a stretched tattoo: I
followed you;
my motion, accumulated stillness, rolled the feeling inside.

We pressed both against memory, one in its left cheek, one in its right;
if either of us moved, we would have touched. Nearness
spoiled everything.

I starved myself with love. You filled up with it. The way you fell
from me:
cautious, exact, grounding my dream with your weight.

Since then, gulls stuffed with cries pass the same fields at
different sunsets;
they have replaced us with younger, more careless ones.
Feeling has tumbled on across those crops smelling of horses;
every time it turned, we had moved, showed our other selves.

The surface tension of our story split where love came in to
make room for us to exit;
dandelions opened when I didn't look, their light kept my gaze down.

Now, another language pricks my throat: a transparent needle;
back home, same blooms wipe my trace with yellow.

Led by empty spaces, your hand, still graceful, takes me every
night to myself.

Elena Tincu-Straton

For You

You are the only one for me
I hope you understand
that when I am alone
I take you by the hand.

You are the greatest friend I know
the one I love so much
and when we are together
how much I need your touch.

You always say the sweetest things
your thoughts are deep in mine
I will never forget you
you are my love divine.

Sometimes we can love
sometimes we can hate
but I always remember
our love was meant as fate.

The first time I saw you
the first loving kiss
I knew we'd be forever
entwined in loving bliss.

And if you ever leave me
I know life will end
because my beautiful darling
you are my lover and best friend.

Tracy Sampson

A Bygone Love

A long time ago, away from here and this life,
My innocent heart fell in love within a hope.
However my sensitive soul was too wary,
And held back my head in telling the world.
So in silent seclusion my heart stood alone,
Whilst my imagination created an unfounded hope.
For the love my heart had to give, would never be returned,
Yet, with some wishing hope, my voice still told the world.
And so upon me the pain of rejection showered down, like the
Piercing hail on a winter's night.
Therefore, will you understand if I keep my heart safe in its case,
And forever only love you from a distance?

M L Courtney

Soul To Speak

A locket in heart and mind
A marvel
Original, only to you and I
A mystic ability
To create superficial reality
Of worlds, past, future, present
Worlds that do not exist
Anything we want to see
Whatever we want to be
Our truth, our spirit, our soul
Seen before our eyes
But, within our mind.
From within us,
But where?
The Atlantis
Of the human brain.

Stephen Tuffnell

INSPIRATION

You are the inspiration I have needed for so long,
I only have to see you and my heart breaks into song.
The world is filled with sunshine when you are here by my side,
And the special joy you bring me when with you I abide.

Surpasses all other feelings that I have felt before,
And in my mind those wonderful memories I will store.
Until again we can be together in an embrace,
When I'll marvel at your gentle touch and your handsome face.

Every word of love I write is written just for you,
You are the only man to whom I always will be true.
All my hopes, desires and longings you completely fulfil,
And deep in my heart I know for sure that you always will.

To have found you at last, after all the time I've waited,
Is like a precious gift with all my fears now abated.
You've banished the loneliness I'd always felt deep inside,
By giving me all the love and passion I'd been denied.

Ann Blair

UNTITLED

Oh Daddy, Daddy.
How we will remember you?
Granddaddy, Granddaddy.
How we will miss you!

Laura Sansom

The Famous Dead

The famous are dying,
So many dead,
We're crying,
We have read about them.

Some dying young,
Some very old,
They were having fun,
Now they are cold.

They want me to tell them
Who's alive and who's dead,
But I only know
From what I've read.

When Diana died
I nearly cried,
The state funeral,
The flowers at the palace,
How the world mourned.

They are dead,
We are alive,
But we're not happy
Because they were part of us.

TV stars, wrestlers,
Boxers, pop stars,
Dead and buried,
Never to be seen again.

It isn't all dull
Because the famous had babies,
People like Pamela and Madonna
And a thousand others.

One dies,
One is born,
Natural progression,
It's inhumane.

Give a thought for the dead,
Not for their money
But for the lives they led.

Alive they were adored,
Dead but not forgotten,
More stars coming
In this age.

Frederick Lewis

FAREWELL

As doubt is speeding once again
Around my troubled mind,
Emotions stir inside my heart
And once again I find
The nights are drawing nearer now,
Remind me of the past,
I'd like to freeze the page of time
For longer and to last.
When will my life be less complete?
Who'll lift this shroud of haze
As I stare out into the night and
Long for better days?
I'm sitting here and wondering
Where do the answers lie?
Would it be fairer to us both
If we could say goodbye?

Kathleen Ross

THE POWER OF LOVE

Whatever it is
The power of love
Will always be strong

Never underestimate
The power of love
It's a wonderful (and true) emotion
That can go up
As well as come down

And it can also hurt . . .
And make you . . .
And break you . . .
And kill you . . .
And torment you . . .

Whatever the case
Love is very strong indeed
It's a very powerful emotion
That can come down
As well as go up
Depending on the situation

Love is a very powerful weapon
That can make you . . .
Or break you . . .
Or kill you . . .
Or torment you . . .
Anything it likes

Never underestimate
The power of love
Whatever it is
Never doubt
The power of it.

John Floyd

BELOVED

He bears a cross for his protection,
With swarthy skin and warm, welcoming eyes
He enchants your heart with his kindness and love
Beckoning you to let him care and soothe your heart and soul.
He is my protector, my love and my all. Without him I am dead
A soulless being bound to walk the Earth alone.
He is my guardian angel although I care for him too.
As soulmates are destined to be together so are we.
Our hearts are entwined together and beating as one,
We are one and without him I crumble.
Weak like a newborn and frail as if ill.
He is my smile, my heartbeat and my angel
My love for him goes on beyond the mortal realm,
My love for him soars into the world
Where children are fearless and roam free
The plane of peace and serenity where soulmates reunite to begin again.
Although he carries illness through life I am his strength as he is mine.
His laughter is my heartbeat and his smile is my breath
His happiness is my blood and without him I cease.
He's like an adult with a mind of a child and a genius
without knowledge
Others respect and look up to him because he is true.
As honest as a child and as thoughtful as an old fashioned romantic
My love for him makes me feel new and special every day.
As exciting and mysterious as the day we met
Our first kiss is as special as when I kiss him now.
As calm as a stream he bears the strength and compassion of a river.
His passion makes my body sing with each touch, each caress
He makes me feel whole and reborn.
There is never silence, as our love cannot be silenced.
My only precious love, my beloved Ben.

Barbara Scott

HAPPY BIRTHDAY

In the year of 1931,
Granma Evans gave birth to a son,
And through his life he fell on hard times,
Upon his brow are worry lines.
Yet he has always been there for me,
The only parent I have known is he.
Mother and Father rolled into one,
He might be 73 but he is still fun.
Hard lessons he has learnt in life,
At 41 he lost his wife.
Mother of his children gone,
30 + years, it seems so long.
Not all his daughters see eye to eye,
But if anything happened they would cry.
But today's your birthday, so have a happy one,
Go and play bingo and have some fun.
On the 19th of February 1931, was the day your life begun,
And on that day they broke the mould,
There could only ever be one Joe.
I have no money to buy a gift, so sorry Father,
It's the first time I have missed,
So I wrote you this poem.
XXX

D Everitt

YOU

I'm sorry to hear that your marriage is through
She can't have loved you the way I do
When you got married you broke my heart
I've loved you from the very start

For many years I've felt this way
Just hoping there might be one day
Will there ever be a chance for me?
Second best didn't work, it never can you see

Secret letters I'd write to you
Then throw them away as I must do
You belong to another and I must wait
Never telling a soul of love's harsh fate

A Valentine card I'd secretly send
But you'd think it a joke when received at your end
So I'll tear it to pieces before it gets out
Feeling foolish and silly and filled full of doubt

But before you throw this note away
Just think what I have had to say
You may be losing the only one
Who is devoted to you her whole life long.

Rosemary Owen

Gallows

I'm hanging from the gallows
For my sins
I'm hanging from the gallows
For my innocence
The crows peck out my eyes
And the rain pours down
And you don't love me anymore

I'm hanging from the gallows
For my strangeness
I'm hanging from the gallows
For my love
Insects crawl on my face
And the full moon shines down
And you don't love me anymore

I'm hanging from the gallows
Underneath the red sky at night
And you don't love me anymore

Geoff Downton

Shine

(For the loving memory of Alma)

Too soon came the day we had to
say goodbye, you have now
become a star in the sky.

There from high above your
spirit will shine, down into
my heart where memory remains alive.

Olli Suntinen

DEVILS AND DESIRE

I am a flaming pit of thrashing emotions.

I am inspired through the pain of the love,
The guilt of desire, the solitude of the deceiver.
And yet I detest these snakes which plague my mind,
I hate the way they twist the truth and hurt the friend.

I am in love with the tender embrace, the fierce passion,
The lustful hope of a lady's kiss.
And yet in this simple act I am robbed of its innocence,
They taint the pure joy and condemn the lonely heart.

I have no morals to judge, I have no honour to save,
I am wicked to the heart, and yet I hurt.
I think I am a good person, I fight these demons.
But they win, I am overrun and subject to their evil.

There seemed but one way to secure success,
To take one's loving heart and tear the tender links,
This done in the name of mortality,
This done so I can stand proud in my pit and defy the Devil.

But I am the Devil and the lover, myself and another,
I am a vessel of emptiness cast into the ocean,
My limbs are tied and I am lost in the grey,
I sink in resignation, no spark on which to float.

I am the cause and the reason, I am to blame.
I desire the passion but I play with fire and I am lost.
Am lost to the flame which I fuel through selfish gain,
I deserve and accept and hate what I am, and yet claim to love.

Chris Smith

When I Think Of You I'll Be Smiling

I remember that last moment
That night when we parted

We sat at the bus stop
I cried, missing you already

The bus drove toward us
I clung to you, frightened

I was lonely already
I'll remember all our good times

I know you can't leave your family
I do understand, I turned to catch the bus

We kissed one last time, goodbye
I saw your tears as I left you

Tomorrow, I begin my new life, I had to leave
Norfolk, they said, is very beautiful

I'll be smiling when I think of you

Carole A Cleverdon

FOR SHARON

There I was on a rain-filled day,
Standing alone, very little to say.
Thinking,
There must be another way.

Confused by all that is real.
No family around,
To love, to hold.

A caring soul is all that I ask,
Someone who cares if I see the morning sun,
A person that knows from this Hell I run,
Someone who sees behind my mask.

Far away I see you, someone who's kind,
Your soul so hard to find,
Sent by angels up above,
Your word so kind, do help me fight!

To Sharon, who be far from my place,
Your words bring joy and hope to my space,
Your kindness and support have helped me along,
You've brought daily smiles to my face.

Laura A Sadler

Betrothed

I bring with me some diamonds,
on a band of pure white gold.
To place upon your finger,
for you to have and hold.
A token of our commitment,
of future life and love.
And hopefully soon, receive a blessing,
from the almighty up above.
Though you may hold this ring precious,
there is much more which I hold dear.
Your eyes, they are my diamonds true,
your hair, my burnished gold,
your lips, my rubies too.
Your hand, it is my setting,
for your heart and soul,
I taketh it in mine,
and know you give it whole.
Your smile, it does awaken,
all the love I hold for you.
May we travel life's sweet journey,
with a love so pure and true.

John James Howarth

Someone Somewhere

Someone somewhere is happy
Someone somewhere is sad
Someone somewhere is dreaming
Of the life they should have had

Someone somewhere is sleeping
Someone somewhere is praying
Someone somewhere is fighting
But they don't know what they're saying

Someone somewhere is hearing a new baby cry
Someone somewhere is grieving a loved one who's died
Someone somewhere is hoping they will get the big win
On some gamble they've made, even though it's a sin!

Someone somewhere makes love, while another makes war
Someone somewhere is bitching of a friend who's a bore
Someone somewhere declares their love for another
And vows to take care of them above any other

So many highs and so many lows
But this world is amazing and it's just
How it goes . . .

Victoria Miller

Rejection

You set your sensual snares for me
and yet I was a willing captive
you were my best friend's wife
but though I was racked with guilt
I gave myself up to the promise of your kiss.

Bodies and minds became so entwined
I thought we would never be unravelled
our flame burned brightly
then you snuffed me out like the proverbial candle
I was left a wreck, floundering on the reef of your ruthlessness.

My friend and you are as one again
and my conscience wants to be glad of it
but my heart is still scolded by your
hard-boiled indifference to my pain.

My words are fuelled by anger but my dreams
are still filled with sweet memories
that will not diminish with the passing of time.

George Holmes

So Cold

As I sit here, my blood runs cold
My ears don't want to hear what I've just been told
Everything stops, everything freezes in time
My thoughts, I don't want them to be mine
My eyes glaze over with a frosty stare
What happens from now on, I no longer care
My voice once warm, has a chilled tone
Will anywhere, ever again, feel like home?
I feel lost and confused, left out in the cold
Now I no longer have you to hold.

Charlotte Watkins

YEARNING

How I wish that I could be
    On a far isle in the sea,
With my friends for company
    A man as well, to pleasure me.

The sun would shine, cool breezes blow
    The wine and laughter soon would flow,
And time itself would pass so slow
    A man as well, to make me glow.

This vision one day could come true,
    The sea so warm, the sky so blue,
The company of friends, and you
    The man who says, 'I love just you'.

Janet P Higgs

APRIL SERENADE

Quietness dwell
In every forest's dell,
Whiffs of mist
Swell between the trees.
Yellowish autumn leaves
Drop to the ground,
The bracken going brownish.
Red berries of the holly,
Their evergreen shiny leaves.
Sorry the birds have gone,
Birds will sing again
Next year their songs
An April serenade
Will dwell in every dell
Sound in every forest glade.

B G Clarke

Please Come

Tormented, torn, my mind in a haze,
The love that I found on those oncoming days,
Did seem to but blossom, I was so unsure
Your eyes dear, did tell me how they littered, the more
Little time did we have, just a glance was its make
You had to tend others and leave me there in the wake
I could have you forever in my heart in anguish,
Cried of endeavour
Was it all a dream that I've wakened to?
In daylight still there all my thoughts are of you
Surrounded by thumping my heart
Your name means so much now that we are apart
Do I have to accept now that we are no more?
Do I walk in silence, talk in grief?
My heart says I love you, my plea in belief.

Hugh Campbell

Rites

He is one, you're other, yet you meet
In middles so absolute that they're all:
Eclipsing extremes without denial,
Embracing differences without regret.
I wish, when you spill out your happiness,
A gin and tonic blue-lit in your hand,
That he could see your eyes, in pain with love,
And hear you feel for words which testify
A future growing from a fleeting past,
Solidifying into certainty.

Today I saw a face that was, I think,
The most beautiful thing I've ever seen.
Witness is experience; but not,
And nothing like, the knowing that you have.

Richard Kitchen

The Precious Asset

Imagine yourself being a multi-billionaire with fat accounts
and lovely mansions but lacking that precious asset.
Imagine yourself ruling the whole world with everything
under your command, but lacking that golden asset.
Imagine yourself flying in your private plane around
the globe at will, but lacking that important asset.

Imagine yourself driven in a bullet-proof limousine with
bodyguards surrounding you, but lacking that golden asset.
Imagine yourself living in paradise where honey
and milk is ever-flowing, but lacking that lovely asset.
Imagine yourself being the richest man on the planet
and enjoying the everlasting life, but lacking the *priceless gift*.

Thank you God for taking your precious time
to mould such a priceless gift, a necessity for mankind.
A woman, an asset no normal man can do without.
Can you do without? I can't.

Thomas Mutangiri

Marie Elizabeth

Baby darling, small and sweet
Mum and Daddy's 'little treat'
Sister to our Emily
Welcome to the family,
May the joy you bring today
Continue all along life's way
And if my wishes do come true
Love and luck will grow with you.
As you watch each day unfurl,
Welcome to your big new world.

A J Langton

THANK YOU

(For Erylene who inspired me to live rather than just exist)

Thank you for your real love and care,
your lovely hugs to remind me that you were there,
the gentle voice with a soft but confident air,
your expressions which always yelled 'I care'
even when we sat quietly in a chair.

Soon we must part for a while,
but whenever I think of you, I will always smile,
value our time previously spent together,
and look forward to coffee in your garden
resplendent in the summer weather.

You gave me so much, and really listened too,
I am very lucky to have met you.
I will think of you often when we are apart,
and you will always live forever in my heart.

Julie Marie Laura Shearing

BOMBSHELL

I knew that things were wrong
When I looked into your eyes.
Their sparkle no longer shone
Then I knew that love had gone,
With no farewells or kiss goodbyes.

Who knows when one's love dies?
Who knows when these things start?
But when you finally realise
It most often takes you by surprise,
A bombshell exploding in your heart.

Keith Tissington

SCULPTURE

I pause and pick more clay from the floor,
As I move I see more, and with greater detail.
The line and form of the neck and shoulder,
The shape of where leg meets buttock, a
Smooth roundness which calms the eye.
    - Such beauty should be seen forever -
I think, I turn and begin to apply more clay
To the basic shape increasing breast,
And round thigh.
'Just hold the pose,' I say, and then turn
Back to my work . . .

David Finlay

OBEDIENCE

My attempts at domesticity
Are integral to my life.
Chores I deemed simplicity
I still consult my wife.
Throw my heart into my cooking,
Careful sharpening a knife.
Get the feeling that she's looking
Just like a caring wife.
We do most things together
Co-joined to combat strife
Throughout all stormy weather,
Me and my loving wife.
But sadly several months ago
She joined the afterlife,
I still seek the approval though
Of my ever-loving wife . . .

Bill Austin

END OF A BEAUTIFUL FRIENDSHIP

Why am I so gullible,
and believe every word he says?
Like declaring his undying love!
Yet will never change his ways!

He says he'd like to take me out,
but his car had broken down!
The car looked alright to me,
I saw him driving it in town!

He apologised profusely!
A new leaf he would turn over,
but I have heard that all before!
He'll always be a rover!

Why am I forgiving,
take him back with open arms?
Because he has such winning ways,
and beguiles me with his charms?

Now he'll be a memory,
as I couldn't take much more!
His eye got blacked and he broke a tooth
when I pushed him through the door!

Greta Gaskin

ONE SHOULD ALWAYS BE IN LOVE

The feelings of 'I'm alive!'
Your emotions take flight
And heart, like a beehive.

The despair of alone
Is no longer your plight,
One less reason to moan.

The sensations of lust
Makes your buttocks clench tight,
'Joy of sex' is a must!

Heat like a liquid rage,
Dims all sensations but sight,
Pulsing beast in a cage.

Dreams become far more real,
Love thoughts of you at night
- Mystifying ordeal!

But just you, being there,
Will you? Won't you? Just might?
That's my heart you can tear.

One should always be in love!

Marty Grief

Butterflies

I'm scared.
Every time I'm round you, I get scared
That I'll do something stupid
And you'll laugh at me.
I'll feel the rushes of blushes
Setting fire to my face.

And I'm nervous
That you'll notice the goosebumps,
Raised dots along my arms,
At the slightest touch from you.
I'll feel the chill of the thrill
Freezing my blood.

But I'm happy
That the butterflies are still there,
Contracting my stomach when you're near,
Fluttering with anticipation.
I'll feel the chill when they're still
And flown.

Danielle Coxon

STILL

Still if I close my eyes
  I can see your smile

(Now and again, you see,
  I dream awhile)

Still I can be with you
  on a summer's day

Still - even though you're a
  thousand miles away.

Locked up inside my heart
  where no one can steal

Memories I shared with you
  (that I *thought* were real).

Thinking - from time to time
  (guess I always will)

Moments I shared with you,
  and remember - still.

Hannah Yates

MOTHER

Never knew how much I loved you,
    or needed you to care.
The thing is Mum, I miss you so,
    now you're no longer there.

I took so much for granted,
    as we very often do.
I seldom took the time to say
    how much that I loved you!

Your love was unconditional
    no matter what I did.
Unwavering and steadfast
    since I was just a kid.

You wouldn't see the faults in me
    although I had a few . . .
and you made me feel that all my dreams
    really could come true!

You guided me in lots of ways,
    for many, many years.
If things went wrong, then you were there
    to wipe away my tears.

I know you're in a better place -
    free from all the pain.
And I love you now and always dear -
    until we meet again!

Maureen Ayling

Remember Me

Remember me, my love, as time goes by,
And as the poppy petals fall, it will bring tears to the eye,
I will be just a memory that lingers on,
And like so many comrades, I too died and was gone.

God guided us to eternal life, you see,
And one day we will meet again in pure eternity,
The battle of war will never end,
And comrades still die, I greet them as a friend.

Old comrades that survived the war,
They have bitter memories of what they saw,
They stand so proud, with medals on their chest,
And say a prayer for those who died, God only takes the best.

Autumn time seems to trigger memory,
The fallen leaves of red and gold fall to the ground you see,
They lay a special carpet, a tribute to those who died, that's true,
And as you walk along, they rustle, maybe God calling you.

Memories are like an open book you see,
See me how I used to be,
Full of life, full of fun,
And I left you, a child whose life has just begun.

I'm deep within that child, you can not see,
And I know that you named him after me,
That's part of me you cannot forget, that's true,
And I look down upon you both, God bless you.

Barbara Holme

TALK TO ME GRANDMA

Grandma, can I sit upon your knee?
I'm hoping you will talk to me
About the past when you were young
And all the things that you have done.
I've heard them many times before
But still I like them more and more.
Times were hard I understand
How hard you worked without your man.
He died when he was thirty-two
Leaving you, two kids and a baby new.
You raised them well and kept your pride,
Remaining loyal from the day he died.
And now you're old it scares me so
I really don't want you to go.
I love your wrinkles and grey hair,
Your double chin and the clothes you wear.
But Grandad's calling you once again,
Together forever you will remain.
Buried in the ground below
I really wish you didn't go.
So I could sit upon your knee,
I wish that you could talk to me.

Audrey Harman

In Memory Of 'Yosser'

Seal-Point Siamese with eyes of blue
I hope you knew how I loved you
You pranced and preened and I was smitten
Right from when you were a kitten
Your bossy ways, the way you talked
The way you purred, the way you stalked
You would butt your head against my chin
And rub yourself against my shin
So quick and agile, full of life
You'd comfort me in times of strife
You seemed to know when I was down
And whirl and dance just like a clown
Gazing into my eyes, face close to mine
Brilliant blue eyes - how they did shine
But then you strayed a little too far
And got run over by a car
The house is empty now you're gone
And Ming still sings his mournful song
He misses you and so do I
While you chase butterflies in the sky

Rose Horscroft

IN A HEARTBEAT

Sweep the words away
With a wave of your hand
Each vowel and consonant falls
Absorbed into the land.

From those letters grew a tree
With shining leaves of gold,
Its branches reaching skyward
To catch the love within its folds.

Deep roots contained the tears
Of many lovers who had found
Their one and only true love
Foundations solid - in fertile ground.

Its heartbeat can be heard
By those who choose to hear
When lying in another's arms
Its beat is crystal clear.

Christina Andrea

The Empty Chair

Light streams from a window
On the bare and empty chair
In a silent corner of my room
Shimmering the air

In that light comes true affection
A warmth and tenderness
Invisible it is not seen
Yet it fills the emptiness

A thought conveyed in astral form
Ethereal through time
Sits upon the empty chair
Always with a smile

From memory's reflection
That love will always shine
Imprinted on the soft folds
Forever in my mind.

Albert Whiteside

MY GRANDMA

How will I remember you?

An opera singer in your prime;

A seamstress -
Able to make a shirt in under 10 minutes;

A 'glamour girl',
Flirtatious and a heartbreaker
Until you met Mr Jagger
(Love at first sight
On a Blackpool fair ride!)
Who became your war hero
After separation in troubled times;

A linguist -
Fluent in Italian and good at German and French;

Generous -
Sneaking me a fiver behind Grandad's back;

Hospitable -
Offering lots of food
And always giving little treats;

A worrier -
Always concerned about the ones you loved;

And although you didn't understand
My lack of interest in sewing and cooking,
You accepted me;

A dancer -
Ballroom dancing until 85 years!

I won't remember you as you were in the end
I'll just remember you saying
'My beautiful Natty'
Even when you could hardly see!

Natalie Jagger

THE KITCHEN TABLE

In my childhood I recall
Our cream scrubbed table, used by all
For many types of household duty,
Made of wood and plain to see.
Heart of our home, my seat was there
On *that* side, by the rocking chair.

We'd hard wooden chairs, with a cushion for me
To raise me higher when we had tea.
Mother kneaded bread sometimes
As I recited nursery rhymes.
Growing up, it was my writing desk,
Or books revealed our world, picturesque.

Homework claimed more serious hours
As I pursued intellectual powers.
Jigsaws teased us for a week
As for the last piece we would seek.
Dad tinkered with the radio set,
Or else clamped on a Ping-Pong set.

Almost a casino on some nights
As card games caused mild family fights.
All that happened, happened *there*,
Even bandaging knees, with Mum's loving care.

It seems to me as we rush about
That families today are missing out,
As they munch quick meals on their knee,
Catching up with the latest TV.
No reaching out to consider each other,
Living for self, not thinking of 'brother'.
How many homes might still be united
If family pow-wows were still ignited?

Margaret Lawley

Dad

Your honesty endeared you to everyone you met,
Your kindness and sincerity we will never forget,
A helping hand for anyone who asked or was in need,
A guarder and a guider in our lives you were indeed.

Words of wisdom you gave for our listening ears,
Gentle yet strong, you could banish our fears.
We know that our lives can never be the same,
Yet the love we have for you will always remain.

Sadly your life we could not save,
Much as we tried to pray,
Only God knows why he took you;
Took you far away,
From our comforting arms and loving hearts,
Left grieving in this way.

The angels are reaching for you,
But we want to hold you tight,
To keep you ever near us;
To say everything's alright

But you must go to Heaven,
With the angels to guide your way,
And know we will always think of you
And reunite some day.

Tracey Lynn Birchall

Blood Brothers

Two blood-splattered faces on our screen
In papers and in magazines.
One bloated by a gunshot wound
Tares, rips, gore all around.

Matted facial hair part of a disguise
Hideous bloodshot eyes
These horrific images on display
In an attempt to drive fear away.

Under their demonic reign
Brutality, abuse, indescribable pain
Mutilations, disfigurements commonplace
Electric shocks, beatings, vanishings without trace.

Playboy psychopaths who sullied all in their path
Whose fun was to rape, carve-up and decap.
Hundreds of thousands vanished without trace
Sons of a murderer born to debase.

Rare was a family not touched by such pain
A brother, a father, some driven insane
Women or children gruesomely murdered too
Recorded on camera for a personal review.

The depths of their depravity will never be released
A chilling story of brothers deceased.

Gloria Hargreaves

The Cold Moon

Five years, and burying the child
seems like yesterday,
a mirror that draws you in
azure as the sea
to which grief runs downriver,
bridge after bridge,
winding towards the deep
as though for some distinct reply,
while your heart scales to an islet
where you anchor for a while
in a different dress
till confusion shifts into chatter,
and the sea, with nothing warm
to touch until it spills
onto a barren stretch of sand, surges.

Grief is the cold moon
splintering with each rage, then
shaking itself whole again,
never staying the same
long enough to mirror
the wilderness within,
the shadowy unbroken ground
of the cold unfrequented woods.
And yet stands in silence
between a loving memory
and the disordered beach
the storm plundered, like you,
caught in between its maze, with
your eyes full of elsewhere,
your dues of a lifetime paid.

Delores Gauntlett

My Love

Your presence is like the light of morning dew
a mirage from a far horizon I never knew
feeling for your touch, our hands meet
frigid, a nun could greet

The days of our youth, mindfully asleep
awaken to our distant heart weep
the sorrow of our lives, (sad) ears to know
our race, our joy, things we own

Our minds, our lives, a burden bear
strange eyes, other worlds unknown, fear
of our lives, the storm through the night
event of our days, that gives the light

In her eyes, the story of our days
the good, the bad, knows our ways
our mind gypsy, taunt, it wanders
to seek and conquer all our anger

A bird, a flight, a song sings
awaken the spirit in us, bliss brings
joy in us, the moment in your bosom
lay, true life between us blossom

Two plain hearts, no motion display
far or near, no distant love delay
even our mind so big and far
cannot our love comprehend, the bar

Frank Xora

Missing You

I miss you so now you are gone
I miss the hours we shared
Your kindness and your loving ways
To show how much you cared
I miss your smile, I miss your voice
That I won't hear again
All these memories I can keep
Though my tears are all in vain
You cannot hear me when I cry
You cannot hold my hand
Shall we ever meet again
In that promised golden land?
There's no answer to the question
But memories linger on
And I shall always love you dear
Until I too am gone.

Lydia Barnett

A Lover's Embrace

We lie here entwined in a lover's embrace
My body relaxed, a smile on my face
Our hearts beating soundly together in time
Me blessing the day that you became mine

A lover's exhaustion consumes us both now
Perspiration beads glistening upon your brow
A moment so tender, so happy, so still
I know that I love you and I always will

We drift off to sleep still together as one
Our passions contented, we've had our fun
Safe in the knowledge that when morning breaks
It will be your face I see when I wake.

Karen Giles

NANA

The little old lady with silver-grey hair,
Her bi-focal specs accompany the chair
in which she sits and knits and sews,
in her twilight she blooms like the perfect rose.
All questions answered without doubt or fear,
and I'll bet without her aid the wrong things she will hear.
She'll growl and look sternly from time to time
if you're 'disrespectful' or you step out of line.
She's proud, honest, forthright and strong,
as gentle as a baby if for you things go wrong.
She has shared a few giggles and fought many wars,
with a smile and a welcome will open her door.
This lady's so special, 'a treasure you see'
to others she's Doris, but Nana to me.

Virginia Aggett

PATCH (THE ONE-EYED DOG)

He lets you know who's boss
He likes to sleep
He likes to doss
Sometimes he gets in a mood
He knows when it's time for his food
Sometimes he gets excited
Sometimes he almost talks
He likes to go out for walks
He's only got one eye
He's hard as nails
He's not afraid to try
He doesn't like going to the vet
He's a one-eyed dog
He's just a pet

Stuart Jackson

MAY

(Dedicated to Mary Shovlin)

How can I describe my friend
hmmm start at the beginning and go to the end

First off she has so many things in common with me
but yet so many things I would not want to be

We became friends right from the start
and very slowly we both have gotten into each other's heart

Let's see a description cannot be put in few words
may a pamphlet, short story or novel or blurb

You see May means a lot to me, more than a billion quid
and if I could turn back time, I'd wish I knew her as a kid

She makes me laugh, and cry, and think, and angry too
but what would friendships be without moody moods?

There have been times I have wanted to tell her off
but we sit on the sofa and work our differences out of love

I guess if I have to say just one thing about May
it's simple, May is about *love* all the way

Anclise Monique

On Wings Of Golden Lust

(Dedicated to Ben, for without him this poem wouldn't have been written)

I first saw you and you shone like radiance.
The colour and power of lightning,
Thunder, driven inside my heart
An earth-shattering silence

From that moment on I knew I loved you,
From the bottom of my heart I do.
Everything about you, perfect to me.
(If there is such a thing as perfection)

With wings of golden lust rising from my soul,
A feeling of the purest trust.
The sun dancing all around you
Could you be the one for me?

I dreamt for the one to save me.
The one whom I would adore.
By my gods, you answered my call,
My love, my life, my all.

And now I know I will not leave you.
For you I give my crimson love.
I'll wrap you up in all that I have.
I want to spend my life with you.

Lucy Kolaj

Old Imitation Leather Handbag

It sat through time
on top of the wardrobe in their bedroom
always there
brown shabby bag

She kept her memories in it
birth certificates and such
a few faded photographs, old earrings, used ration books

seemed old fashioned to me, as a child
I suppose it was forties in style
with a broken clasp
worn out from past use

I was loved as a child
I just knew, as you do
safe and steady, at the centre of my universe

that my parents loved each other I believed,
Mum and Dad, rock solid, sound
but I never saw them kissing or any of that stuff
when I was around

She died first, gone
before I was ready to meet her through adult eyes
and he had carried on
as people do, making the best of it
muddled through the years alone

After he'd passed
clearing, sorting to do
I took the bag down and spilled open inside
old imitation leather handbag with secrets to hide
so many letters they'd written,
love letters throughout the war,
showing, teaching me just who they were

My parents,
who never kissed before me
were Romeo and Juliet,
a Cathy and Heathcliffe, passionate
briefly encountering in their time

pretty endearments whispered intimately over the page,
young wartime lovers, strangers to me
I read their letters discovering, lovingly
then put them away, inside the bag

that now sits through time
on top of my wardrobe in the bedroom
always there
brown shabby bag

Hilary Walker

Family Values

I didn't do very much today.
Just stayed at home and helped David play.
We built a castle and won a battle.
We drove 'round the farm, counting our cattle.
We painted a picture (and some of the walls).
We played in the garden; threw and caught balls.
We ate our lunch and had a nap.
We watched some telly - David in my lap.
We counted to ten with some coins in the shop.
We bought an ice lolly or two (one got dropped).
We sang and danced to some nursery rhymes.
We swung on the swing and slid down the slide.
We built a den with some sheets and some pegs.
We tiptoed, we marched and hopped on one leg.
I had a great time, helping David to play,
but I didn't do much that is valued today;
except by David and me, I'd say.

K B Newbrook

Missing You

I am looking up at the stars
I know you're looking up as well
And I wonder where you are now
Because I miss you

I can feel the cold night
It is wrapping around me
Just like your arms used to do
Now I'm so cold, because I miss you

The moon is glowing so bright
Shining down upon me
Just like your eyes used to do
Now I'm blinded and I miss you

I am empty without you
All life's meaning walked away
All I have now is your memory
And I shall miss you until the day I die

Mark Anthony Games

My Little Sister

My little sister likes smacking
She smacks everyone
She doesn't care
She writes on the wall
She scribbles everywhere
She wrote on Cynthia's bed
She touches yucky stuffs
And licks them
But she's *my sister . . .*

Prescilia Nkani (7)

As One

We were as one in the beginning
Until life forced us apart.
Many grew the miles between us
Yet I kept you in my heart.
Through the changing of the seasons,
Through summer breeze and howling gale,
Our paths continued to meander
As we traversed hill and dale.
Sadly I've missed so many milestones
That have been scattered on your way,
Missed the sunshine and the shadows
That seem to make up every day.
My life has turned so many corners
Whilst broken hearts I've had a few
But no matter where I wander,
Every road leads back to you.

Rosemary Thomson

Missing You

Remembering in my heart
You were pure gold
Crying a river of tears
Adored and never far away
Breath in my body breathing in the memory
Laughing and having fun
When it is over the divide is there
Missed and adored for evermore.

Olive M Poole

To The Memory Of Your Soul

Beyond the raging desert
To the coolness of the sea
Lies a love I once lived for
And she's waiting there for me.

From the valley of the forgotten
To the memory of your soul
Love danced around in circles
And left my heart at home.

Across the seamless sky
Along to the shore of stones
There I found my love
Sleeping by the door.

The love we shared together
Is the same as long ago
And my heart will rejoice forever
To the memory of your soul.

B G Ryan

Missing You

The phone sits brooding
Silently longing to ring,
No key scrapes the lock,
Seconds echo into days,
Nights are black voids without you.

Smiling from its frame
Your photograph watches me
Listening for your voice,
The house holds its breath, hoping
For your footsteps on the path.

Valerie Sutton

Love

This all consuming passion
This thing called love
It lets you do so many things
It lets you rise above

And you never can know
Just really how far
When you stand on tiptoe
And reach for that star

I feel all giddy
Am I really this girl?
I hear his voice
I'm in such a whirl

His voice like chocolate
Makes me melt
The touch of his hands
Like this, never felt

A love so unconditional
That we had found
Not meant to last
I'll be bound!

But times we had
In memory forever
Cannot be deleted
Not now, not ever

Simone C Summerscales

LIFE AND DEATH

The day before I loved you
Was the day before I died
I've died of the longing for you
But did I live before I died?

I died on the day I loved you
It was the day before I died
I live only for the longing of you
Will this longing never die?

I want the longing of you
Will die if it's not there
I need the crying for you
If I'm not to despair

I cannot live without you!
I don't want to die alone
Will you die of longing for me?
A long long way from home

If I meet you on the morrow
Will I live before I die?
I'm fearful of the morrow
In case you say goodbye.

Pluto

Dearest Clone - A Mother's Promise

My daughter, your transparency is showing
My sister, I can read your tiny mind
In dreams I see your teenage cheeks are glowing
In your bedside table my own memories I find.

To bridge your troubled soul while you are growing
To smooth your way of obstacles I knew
In waters deep and still, not overflowing
Your life I'll guard, our instincts will be true.

No tide will drown you while I span the ocean
No abyss of fear to swallow or to hold
No man will threaten, flooding with emotion
My love is yours to strengthen and enfold.

Your stepfather has left us close together
To be your brother-in-law he could not bear
Enough to know being all to one another
One flesh shall be our certainty to share.

Skin of my skin, blood of my own creation
Heart of my heart and bone cell of my bone
Our future holds the founding of a nation
One mind, bridge, anthem, children of the clone.

Christopher Payne

A Letter Of Love

A letter of love from a kind-hearted friend
Is something to treasure to life's very end;
For it speaks with affection that still will live on,
Cherished forever when this life has gone.

A letter of love will lift a drooped head,
And stiffen the spine, and put spring in the tread,
Will gladden the soul, and enrapture the mind,
And help make life brighter, more joyous, more kind.

A letter of love that is written sincere
Has short, gentle words that fall soft on the ear,
And words that encourage and strengthen in spring
The same joys in autumn and winter will bring!

A letter of love, like a white-winged dove,
Brings God's sweet blessings from Heaven above;
It speaks words of courage, of faith, hope and peace,
And boldly asserts God's love will not cease!

Dan Pugh

Faith, Someday - RIP

That day I lost you I didn't want to live,
To accept you were gone, I couldn't believe.
Two years to the day, and I still miss you,
I sit at your grave and don't know what to do.
You were my baby, all I ever wanted,
I hope you heard every word of love I said.
I lay flowers on your grave, to let you know how much
you meant to me,
I look at your photos and pray you were here with me.
Lying on the floor, tears falling from my face,
I knew nothing or no one could ever replace
What you meant every single day to me,
I want you in my arms, not away from me.
I love you and I always will,
You were my faith and we'll be together again.
Rest in peace baby,
When I'm with you again, that will save me.
I'll never forget you or forget that day,
Wait for me darling; I'll be with you again someday.

Sarah Sproston

NEVER SIMPLE YET NEVER PLAIN

I close my eyes
Listen
And open the doors
To let you in
I never have before
Is it cold
I feel it in my skin
This imagination is a sin
Memories like old movies
Come to life
Come to me
Once so plain, yet
Please don't damage
Don't change
What doesn't fit in
Give nature a chance to win
This is the part when simple roads
Become up hill struggles
So ruined, ruined
By one of us, who?
Many times, so many times
Again
And again
Till one of us will finally change.

Bryony Freeman

INFORMATION

We hope you have enjoyed reading this book - and that you will continue to enjoy it in the coming years.

If you like reading and writing poetry drop us a line, or give us a call, and we'll send you a free information pack.

Alternatively if you would like to order further copies of this book or any of our other titles, then please give us a call or log onto our website at www.forwardpress.co.uk

Anchor Books Information
Remus House
Coltsfoot Drive
Peterborough
PE2 9JX
(01733) 898102